Pâtés and Terrines

Pâtés &
Terrines
Sheila Hutchins

Elm Tree Books · London

First published in Great Britain 1978
by Elm Tree Books/Hamish Hamilton Ltd
90 Great Russell Street London WC1B 3PT

Some of the recipes included in this volume
originally appeared in *Pâtés, Terrines and Things*
joint copyright © 1976 by Sheila Hutchins and
Grants of St James's Publications

Illustrations by Alan Cracknell

British Library Cataloguing in Publication Data

Hutchins, Sheila
    Pâtés and terrines.
    1. Pâtés (Cookery)   2. Terrines (Cookery)
    I. Title
    641.6'6   TX773
    ISBN 0-241-89892-7

Photoset and printed in Great Britain by
Lowe & Brydone Printers Limited, Thetford, Norfolk

Notes on the recipes

Ingredients have been listed in both metric and imperial (in brackets) measures. It is most important to follow one set of measurements or the other, as they are not exact conversions. Liquid measures actually convert at ½ pint = 280 ml and 1 pint = 560 ml; these have been rounded up in all cases to 300 and 600 ml.

Wherever the symbol * appears with a recipe, it indicates that the dish is particularly economical, and good value for money.

If you would like to make pâtés and terrines at home and then sell them to people you should write to the National Federation of Women's Institutes, 39 Eccleston Street, Victoria, London SW1 9NT and ask them for their N.F.W.I. Market Handbook. It is full of useful information on selling home-made food of all sorts in W.I. markets. You do not have to be a member to do this. They also point out that their Market Handbook details various regulations concerning fish and meat spreadable products and that these cover pâtés. A lot of their markets sell pâtés and terrines and they are very popular. They tell me they 'have an understanding with the Health Authorities that anyone producing this type of goods for the market can have their kitchen inspected at any time by the Health Authorities. According to the regulations kitchens should be registered but obviously it would be impossible to register all the W.I. kitchens producing for the markets so we are very careful to see that hygiene is observed.'

Introduction

'My idea of heaven,' said the Reverend Sidney Smith, 'is eating *pâté de foie gras* to the sound of trumpets.' This very witty and humane nineteenth-century parson much enjoyed the good things of life, but the Victorians said that he had a frivolous attitude to it and would never make a bishop. Neither did he. Though today few of us can afford *pâté de foie gras* very often, there are dozens of excellent pâtés, terrines and related dishes which are very easy to make, inexpensive and perhaps even better accompanied by a bottle of red or white wine than by the sound of trumpets.

Nowadays pâtés, galantines and even mousses can be made from almost anything from snipe and woodcock, hares and rabbits, to wild boar or kippers, and they are very fashionable. The restaurant Laserre in Paris does a terrine full of eels, and I have tasted a *pâté d'anguilles aux ortilles,* an eel pâté flavoured with nettles, at a hotel in the Belgian Ardennes. This is not incidentally nearly so strange as it may seem; nettle broth was a springtime delicacy on farms in Ireland during a great part of the nineteenth century, and nettles, if picked young, do not taste prickly when cooked. In the Belgian province of Hainault they make a *pâté de lievre à la Dupin* with hand-chopped pork, hare's blood and fillets of hare mixed with red wine and pickled gherkins; elsewhere, larks and thrushes are preserved whole in clarified butter in little potting pots and flavoured with juniper berries. There is even a pâté made in Corsica from the local blackbirds stewed in wine, brandy and 'spirits of myrtle', an experience to be missed.

In this book I have included some of the recipes that I have collected at various times in France, Belgium and elsewhere, and I have also put in one or two things such as *brandade de morue* and Hungarian *Liptoi* which, though not really pâtés at all, can be eaten on much the same occasions. They are also very good. I have included, too, a few of the lovely old recipes for English potted meat, of which I am very fond and which I think has been undeservedly forgotten. You will probably find them, as a house speciality, in your local wine bar the week after next!

If you have never made pâtés or terrines you probably do not realize how inexpensive they can be. The majority of them will feed a large number of people at little cost and most of them are perfect cold buffet food, justly popular for parties. They should be well chilled and are delicious in sizzling weather served on cracked ice with crisp radishes or black olives. They can be made in advance and good pâté should not really be eaten for two or three days after it has been cooked, so as to give it time for the flavours to develop. Very few pâtés or terrines freeze well—the flavour seems to fade and the texture to go wishy-washy—but they keep quite well for a week or so in the refrigerator and indeed the old classic pâtés, drained of their own stock and sealed from the air with a thick layer of lard, were designed to be kept for two or three months in a cool larder. It was an old-fashioned method of preserving food for winter.

They make an excellent beginning for a formal meal, and some are very good as a main dish, perhaps with hot jacket potatoes and a plain salad tossed in oil and lemon juice, while on a hot day a simple meal of home-made pâté and bread can be completely satisfying and is a perfect foil to a bottle of red wine. You really need nothing more; most French pâtés are so rich one needs no butter with them.

Traditionally, a lot of *pâtés de campagne* were made at the time of the autumn pig-killing, when hams were salted down for Christmas and Easter and some of the offal and bits and pieces were packed into sausage skins for Martin-mass, the Feast of Sausages and Gut Puddings, on 25th November. Other bits were made into pâtés and there would be huge bowls, or *terrines,* full of delicious pâté sealed with lard, in the cellars and larders of every respectable farmhouse or château beside the bottled fruits and ripening cheeses.

Pâtés are still commonly preserved in tightly-sealed glass jars, like bottled fruit, in country places all over France. They need about two hours' cooking, and it is a good way of keeping the pâté, which, in its glass preserving jar, has a charming grandmotherly appearance. I tasted some delicious pâté of this type last summer in the Haute Savoie, in a high Alpine valley near the Lac des Confins, at the home of a farmhouse cheese-maker. Regretfully I have given no recipes for this method of preserving pâtés, however, as the rubber rings which have to go on preserving jars are almost impossible to get in this country now.

In southwest France, particularly in the Dordogne and the Perigord districts, where they specialize in rearing geese and ducks specially fattened by force feeding, the goose and duck meat is cooked in its own fat and preserved in earthenware jars. *Confit d'oie*, or preserved goose and *confit de canard*, or preserved duck, are among the oldest French traditional dishes widely used in family kitchens and invented before the days of refrigeration as a means of preserving the birds. Nowadays they are also obtainable in tins. *Confit* should be simply served: as it is, with the fat removed (so that it is not too rich and heavy), cold with a green salad; or hot—the pieces of *confit* covered in their fat may be heated in a fireproof earthenware dish in a moderate oven until they are a light golden colour with the skin lightly browned and the meat soft. Hot *confits* are traditionally served with white haricot beans, or fried *cèpes* (mushrooms) cooked with garlic, or buttery peas, or peeled sliced potatoes fried in goose fat, with added garlic and parsley. This is one of those simple things, like the art of making good tea, which requires skill and practice for the best results. The *foies gras* or fatted goose livers from these specially reared geese and ducks are sold at markets and fairs in Alsace and the Perigord district from 15th November to the end of December.

One must distinguish of course between the *pâté de foie gras*, or prepared and truffled pâté, and the fresh fatted goose and duck livers from which it is made. Nowadays the demand is so great that about fifty per cent of the *foie gras* handled annually in France comes from abroad, mostly from Hungary and other central European countries. The Hungarians cook them deliciously in milk. In France they are baked in the oven but eaten cold, not iced, at the beginning of a meal when the palate is fresh. *Foie gras* is traditionally served pink. Warm toast is served, or fresh French bread, and there is endless argument about what to drink with it. Opinions vary between champagne, a good red burgundy, well-chilled

Gewurtztraminer or Château d'Yquem. I have given no recipes for these things as the *foie gras* is unobtainable here.

The inimitable *pâté de foie gras de Strasbourg* was invented in 1765 by Monsieur Close, chef to the military governor of Alsace, the Maréchal de Contades. M. Close remained in Alsace when the Maréchal left, married a *pâtissier's* widow, and, having kept his recipe secret, made the *pâté de foie gras en croûte* a speciality of their shop. He also made a fortune and was much copied. The now familiar truffles were added later by a chef from the Perigord.

The French word *pâté* means paste. *Pâte,* the same but without the second accent, means pastry. Our own words patties and patty pans as well as paste and pastry all come from the same ancient source, the Latin *pasticium*. It is a root which has given masses of words to the French, English and Italian languages: pastry-cook, *pâtissier* and the Italian *pasta* for instance.

All pâtés must originally have been baked in pastry crusts, but then it was found that they kept much longer when they were baked in a dish and sealed off from the air with lard or butter. This was of great importance to the skilled *charcutiers* who often had orders for their special pâtés from all over France. So they began to bake them in earthenware dishes, called *terrines*, which could be sent by *diligence* or stage coach, with the pâté in it, at little extra cost. They became more and more popular and gradually the pâté took its name from the thing it was cooked in (rather as the Irish talk of 'having a jar' when they are really referring to the contents). Now the names pâté and terrine are almost interchangeable.

Soon terrines became so popular that potteries began to make fireproof dishes to look like meat pies for people to make their pâtés in. They became fashionale both here and in France and both Spode and Wedgwood made terrines— or tureens as the English sometimes called them—in this 'piecrust pottery' which now fetches vast prices in the saleroom.

In England the old word tureen, now usually thought of in connection with soup, was once used to describe dishes for potted meat and is evidently an anglicized form of the word terrine. It has been used from time to time since the seventeenth century at least. Patrick Lamb (chief cook at St James's Palace from the reign of Charles II to Queen Anne)

10

wrote that a 'terryné-dish at Court' was made of silver 'round and upright, holding about six quarts English measure or three pint-and-a-half Scotch measure, with two handles such as a small cistern has'. There were Mittoons and Puptons too, made at the English Court in those days, which were evidently not unlike a modern terrine.

English *pâtés en croûte,* or raised pies, were once very elaborate, containing all kinds of game, poultry or meat— perhaps a whole goose, capercailzie or York ham, boned and stuffed with tongue, truffles, and so on. They were at one time a great speciality of the hunting shires and have been popular in England since the middle ages at least, when the citizens of London used to buy them hot from the pastry cooks at Pye Corner. They are commemorated not only in Chaucer and elsewhere but in the nursery rhyme of Simple Simon who met a pieman going to the fair. He was still a familiar figure in Victorian England.

'The itinerant trade in pies is one of the most ancient street callings of London. The meat pies are made of beef or mutton; the fish pies of eels; the fruit of apples, currants, gooseberries, etc . . .,' as Henry Mayhew wrote in *London Labour and the London Poor* in 1851. 'At the public houses a few pies are sold, and the pieman makes a practice of "looking in" at all the taverns on his way. Here his customers are found principally in the tap-room. "Here's all 'ot!" the pieman cries as he walks in. "Toss or buy! Up and win 'em!" This is the only way that the pies can be got rid of: "If it wasn't for tossing we shouldn't sell one". To "toss the pieman" is a favourite pastime with costermongers' boys and all that class; some of whom aspire to the repute of being gourmands, and are critical of the quality of the comestible. If the pieman wins the toss, he receives 1d. without giving a pie: if he loses, he hands it over for nothing. "Gentlemen out on the spree at the late public houses will frequently toss when they don't want the pies, and when they win they will amuse themselves by throwing the pies at one another, or at me".'

Nowadays a lot of French and Belgian pâtés are commercially made, instead of by the housewife or local *charcutier.* They are often vacuum packed with the traditional earthenware pots or glass preserving jars with check gingham covers sealed inside the transparent packing. They are also becom-

11

ing more and more elaborately and sometimes ill-advisedly garnished. For they can now be sold straight from the pot in refrigerated cabinets. The customer can see what it is, the mouth waters, and there are fancy garnishes set in aspic or other jelly of various colours—these may be anything from a piece of pineapple or glacé cherry to an orange, bay leaf or chilli peppers. Rumour has it that some chefs now pass them off as *pâté maison,* or chef's special. It is much better, as well as cheaper, to make them yourself.

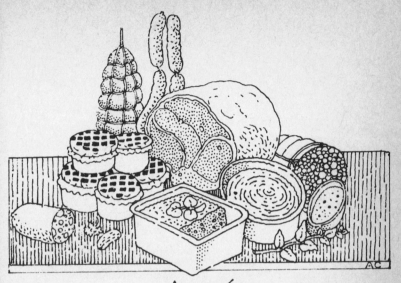

PÂTÉS

THE SIMPLE *pâtés bourgeois* and *pâtés ménagère* made by French housewives perhaps once or twice a week are usually not at all complicated or expensive to prepare. They are all highly individual, for the recipes vary not only in different regions but from one village to another. In some parts of France they make them in pastry cases, in others they do not. Some are pounded to a purée with a pestle and mortar, or sometimes with an electric mixer, others are coarsely minced. Some are simply chopped by hand with a kitchen knife. It makes a great difference not only to the texture but also to the flavour of the finished pâtés. Sometimes the different textures are mixed in layers. Some pâtés, by the way, look impossibly rich when they come hot from the oven and may well be swimming in fat and juices from the meat. Do not be daunted, as the pâté will look very different when cold; the fat is there partly to cook and partly to preserve the meat. You do not eat the lard on top.

Pâtés are best made two or three days before they are to be eaten so the flavours can develop. They keep about ten days under refrigeration, rather less in a cool larder. Pâtés topped with aspic or any jelly keep less well than those covered with lard or butter. If the pâté is to be kept for ten days or more in the refrigerator, unmould it after chilling, wipe off the meat jelly, and put it back in its pot covered with melted lard to seal off the air.

Few pâtés freeze well. This is immediately obvious when one tastes them. The damp quality of a once frozen, thawed-out pâté is unmistakable.

The minced meat mixture in a pâté is called forcemeat, stuffing or farce in English, and *farce* in French. Its connection with a dramatic work intended to excite laughter is obscure, but real. The word *farce* comes from the Latin *farcire* to stuff, and was used metaphorically for the (comic) interludes which padded out meatier performances.

15

For meat that should be chopped, hold the knife blade by both ends and chop with a rapid up and down movement. Brush the ingredients into a heap, again and again, with the knife. Do not economize on kitchen knives—they should be very sharp and the best available. I use French chefs' knives made by Sabatier or Swiss butchers' knives made by Victorinox, and I thrust the sharp pointed ends into corks in the kitchen drawer, like fencing foils.

The electric mixer gives a fine textured purée similar to that of the old-fashioned pestle and mortar, and is much used by *charcutiers*.

Liver is less unpleasant to mince at home if one slices it and fries it very lightly first in butter. Some butchers are unwilling to mince anything but beef in their large commercial mincers. They say other mixtures would get mixed with the beef and that the mincer would have to be dismantled and cleaned afterwards, but other butchers are pleased to do this. In comparing English butchers unfavourably to those in France one should, all the same, remember that French butchers and fishmongers are usually tipped for these special services—boning, filleting, skinning, mincing and tying up their wares in some special shape, but English butchers are not.

In pâtés and terrines, strips of attractive looking meat and fat that have been marinated in gin, sherry, port or cognac are often arranged in layers with the forcemeat, and look very interesting when the finished dish is cut. This is what chefs call a *salpicon*.

Coarse-cut Pâté from the Ardennes

The small *charcutiers'* shops in the Ardennes in Belgium often have superb pâtés made on the premises, sometimes to their own secret recipe. They also specialize in many different and delicious sausages, black and white puddings and hogshead 'cheese'—a sort of brawn—as well as the famous local hams which are often dry salted by a member of the family in the cellar below the shop. These hams are mostly eaten raw in wafer-thin slices for 'starters', though they can be cooked.

This is a mild but coarsely textured pâté from the Hotel de la Poste, Bouillon, in the Belgian Ardennes.

For the pâté one needs 225 g (8 oz) each of fresh pork, fatty pork belly, chicken liver and veal. Chop it all together as finely as possible with a large kitchen knife held level. Do not mince the meat, as you will spoil the texture of this pâté. Add a coffee spoon of salt, a coffee spoon of pepper, a raw egg, and 2 tablespoons of cognac or rum or Madeira. Mix it well together and pack it into a fireproof terrine or dish. Lay a bay leaf, some sprigs of fresh thyme, and rashers of bacon on top. Cover it with foil. Stand the dish in a tin of enough warm water to come halfway up the sides, and cook in a moderate oven, 180°C (350°F)/Gas 4, for 1 hour. Remove the foil during the last twenty minutes.

To be served chilled as a first course, or for a party with hot crisp toast.

Pâté Bourgeois au Lapin

A coarse-cut rabbit pâté popular in northwest France, this recipe was given to me some years ago by a Calais shopkeeper. It is delicious, and unusual in being marinated in beer. One can drink red or white wine with it.

Put 900 g (2 lb) of chopped boned rabbit and 300 ml (½ pint) of beer such as light ale in a basin. Add 450 g (1 lb) of pork belly, chopped and without the skin, 3 bay leaves, a little thyme and parsley, and some salt and pepper. Leave it overnight, then mince the pork and rabbit separately. Line a fireproof dish with bacon rashers, pack the minced meat in it in layers, and pour the beery liquor into it. Cover with foil and a lid and bake the pâté for 2½-3 hours in a slow oven, 150°C (300°F)/Gas 2. Cool.

Pâté de Foie aux Pruneaux*

A coarse-cut country pâté from the north of France. It is still made in Flanders and contains prunes as well as fat bacon.

Chop 350 g (12 oz) of fat bacon (without the rind) and 450 g (1 lb) of pig's liver coarsely together. Add a very little salt, some freshly ground black pepper and 100 g (4 oz) of roughly chopped prunes, weighed after they have been soaked and stoned. Add 2 tablespoons of brandy. Mix well, pack it all into an earthenware terrine, cover the top with rashers of bacon and thinly sliced onion rings. Put a lid on the terrine. Bake it in a slow oven, 150°C (300°F)/Gas 2, for 1¾ hours. When cooked, cover the top of the terrine with foil or waxed paper and cool the pâté under weights by putting a saucer or small plate and some kitchen weights on top. It is served sliced in the terrine.

Liver Pâté with Hazelnuts

In Normandy, with its lush water meadows, many apple orchards and rich soft cheeses such as Camembert and Livarot, they cook nearly everything in cream and sometimes with Calvados as well. The pâtés there are very rich, too, and should be served well chilled. One does not normally need butter with them. This pâté would be enough for ten or more people when served cold—chilled—as a first course with a crusty French loaf or with a fresh baked warm English cottage loaf, and perhaps some large pickled gherkins or big crisp garden radishes. It also makes a good main course with a tossed salad and hot jacket potatoes.

The large quantity of fat in this recipe is intentional. When baked with less fat, both the flavour and texture of the finished dish are spoiled. You need 450 g (1 lb) of pig's liver and 375 g (12 oz) of unsalted pork belly without the skin. Ask the butcher to chop both of them finely. If your butcher is unresponsive, then put it quietly through the mincer (coarse plates) when you get it home. Mix the chopped liver and chopped pork belly with 225 g (8 oz) lard, some salt, pepper, a small peeled chopped garlic clove, 3 tablespoons of water and 3 tablespoons of Calvados (this is distilled in Normandy from cider apples but I use whisky instead when it is unavailable). Now add 100 g (4 oz) of shelled unsalted hazelnuts (from health stores and good grocers). Let it stand for an hour before packing it into a big earthenware pot.

Cover the top with a piece of fat pork or of lacey flead fat, then top it with foil. Bake it in a slow oven, 150°C (300°F)/Gas 2 for 2½-3 hours. Let it get cold before putting it away, in the refrigerator. It should not really be eaten for two or three days after it has been cooked.

Fromages d'Italie*

This has nothing to do with Italy and is not a cheese either; it is the old French name for a good household pâté. Like many old-fashioned household pâtés this one is wrapped in a *crépine*—a piece of flead, caul fat or veiling (see the note under Faggots, page 113). Since people here are sometimes unsure what this is, English recipes often specify thin bacon rashers for wrapping pâtés instead. This is good but the taste is a little different and it is worth trying to get the flead fat from the butcher.

Dice, mix and then mince 225 g (8 oz) of pork belly (without the rind or bones) and 675 g (1½ lb) of pig's liver. Soak 225 g (8 oz) breadcrumbs in 200 ml (⅓ pint) of boiling milk, add salt, squeeze out the milk, mash the breadcrumbs to a paste and spread this on a buttered plate. Add it cold to the meat and blend it to a purée in the electric liquidiser. Mix well. Season the mixture with pepper, salt, half a teaspoon of freshly grated nutmeg, half a teaspoon of ground cloves, a little thyme, sage and chopped parsley.

Put the flead fat or veiling in a basin of warm water for a few minutes. Then pull out the pieces to make a lacy veil of fat, and use to line the bottom and sides of a terrine, leaving enough to fold over the top. Put the pâté mixture in the middle. Cover the top with veiling, a slice of back fat, a piece of greaseproof paper, and finally a lid. Stand the dish in a tin filled with enough hot water to come halfway up the sides. Bake it in a moderate oven, 180°C (350°F)/Gas 4, for about 2 hours. When cooked let the pâté get cold and then unmould it by dipping the lower part of the terrine in boiling water for an instant, being careful to get none of it in the pâté. Then reverse it on to a plate, removing the caul or veiling only as the pâté is eaten for it protects the outside.

The recipe comes from *La Cuisine à l'Usage des Ménages Bourgeois*, by Baron Brisse, who was a journalist and author of several fashionable cookery books between 1860-1875 and a well-known figure in nineteenth-century Paris. People said, however, that he had a 'romantic', frivolous attitude to food like that of Alexandre Dumas in *Le Grand Dictionnaire de Cuisine*. 'The disappearance of the hot hors d'oeuvre is the result of the excessive development of women's skirts,' Baron Brisse wrote in *La Liberté* in 1866, when enormous crinolines were fashionable. 'In a properly administered household, the overexpenditure on one side has to be balanced by economies on the other.'

Pâté de Cervelle de Veau

An elegant summer pâté which tastes subtly of tarragon, this is made with eggs, brains and fresh green herbs and is enough for twelve people. Calves' brains are the most delicate but are often difficult to find in British shops. Lambs' brains, though not quite so good, might be substituted.

Peel and chop 2 onions as fine as possible. Put them in a pan with 2 tablespoons of chopped parsley, 1 tablespoon of chopped fresh tarragon, and 2 tablespoons of chopped fresh chervil. Add a generous 150 ml (¼ pint) of oil and let the herbs simmer in it gently for 5 minutes.

Having prepared 450 g (1 lb) of calves' brains by soaking them in cold water with a little lemon juice or white vinegar for an hour, drain and trim them, and rinse them in fresh cold water. Poach them in boiling salted water for 5 minutes. Drain them thoroughly, add them to the herb mixture with 450 ml (¾ pint) of water, some salt and pepper. Let them simmer uncovered until all the water has disappeared. Slice the brains in large pieces.

Beat 12 eggs until the yolks and white are well blended, then add 3 tablespoons of chopped pistachio nuts. Mix everything together. Oil a warmed mould or large soufflé dish, pour in the mixture, and bake it in a moderate oven, 180°C (350°F)/Gas 4, for 15 minutes. Unmould when cold.

The pâté may be garnished with parsley or watercress and crisp fresh radishes.

Pâté de Faisan

Here is one of those French country pâtés which are served all over France with gherkins or black olives or with crisp garden radishes and freshly baked bread. Recipes vary from village to village but the pâtés usually appear at lunchtime at the start of the meal, to replace the good household soup which is nowadays mostly kept for the evening meal. This recipe is from a village in central France. Smoked Morvan ham and *boudin au Serpollet* (a black pudding flavoured with wild thyme) are other local specialities, as well as Crottin de Chavignol and Valmeuse cheeses.

Bone and chop a raw pheasant, setting aside the liver. Mix the chopped pheasant with 350 g (12 oz) lean pork belly or other chopped lean pork. Brown the mixture gently in 50 g (2 oz) lard and put it *once* through the mincer, coarse plates.

Mix 100 g (4 oz) chicken liver with the pheasant's liver, trim and chop them roughly and brown them in the lard together with 2 peeled, finely chopped garlic cloves and 3 peeled, very finely chopped shallots. Stir in 1 tablespoon of brandy and then put this mixture *twice* through the mincer, fine plates. Mix it with the coarsely minced pork and pheasant, adding salt, pepper, chopped parsley, powdered thyme and a bay leaf. Stir in a glass of red wine and pack it into a terrine or fireproof dish.

There should be enough liquid to rise about 0.5 cm (¼ in) above the mixture. Add more wine if necessary. Cover the terrine or dish with foil. Bake it in a moderate oven, 180°C (350°F)/Gas 4, for about 30 minutes, then reduce the heat to 170°C (325°F)/Gas 3 and continue to bake it uncovered for about 1½ hours till it is fairly dry and the top is brown and crusty. The exact time depends on the shape of the dish in which it is cooked.

Pâté de Foie de Porc Ménagère*

Chop 450 g (1 lb) pig's liver and 450 g (1 lb) lean unsalted pork together with a kitchen knife held at both ends. This takes a little time to do but the texture of the pâté is just as important as the seasoning. Add salt, pepper, ground cloves and freshly grated nutmeg. Mix well and divide it in four portions. Line the bottom of a round terrine with a layer of thin, rindless unsmoked bacon rashers. Put in a layer of the minced mixture, then one of bacon, then another of minced mixture and so on till you have used all the minced meat. Finish with a layer of bacon. (You will need approximately 350 g (12 oz) bacon, depending on the size of the dish.) Put a bay leaf on top of it, and cover the dish tightly with foil and a lid. Stand it in a baking tin filled with enough warm water to come halfway up the sides, and bake in a slow oven, 150°C (300°F)/Gas 2, for 3½ hours. Do not remove lid until the pâté is very cold. It may be served in the terrine or unmoulded.

This pâté can be made with pickled pork belly instead of bacon.

Kipper Pâté*

Put two kippers heads down in a jug of boiling water. After 5 minutes, fish them out by the tails and remove the skins, and large and small bones. Make a purée in the electric blender with the kippers, 75-100 g (3-4 oz) softened butter, the juice of 1 lemon, a pinch of Cayenne pepper, some freshly grated nutmeg and 1 tablespoon of thick cream. Pack the pâté into an earthenware jar, and store it in the refrigerator.

Gehatkeh Leber*

The Jewish chopped liver paste is very simple and quick to prepare. It is delicious spread on little biscuits.

Fry 225 g (8 oz) of chopped onions in poultry fat, then trim 450 g (1 lb) of chicken livers and grill them gently until no longer pink. Put the liver and onions through the mincer together with three shelled hard-boiled eggs. Add salt and pepper to taste.

In Hungary, much of central Europe, and in southwest France, a great deal of the cooking is done in goose fat, which gives a subtle flavour to the food. It has a low melting point, delicate taste and also makes first-rate pastry. Sold here by some butchers and poulterers, it may have to be rendered down before use.

Little Pots of Liver Paste (Var)

The pâté is used to fill small glass jars which should be topped with foil and may be stored for about a week in the refrigerator. In France, before they are brought to the table, the tops of the jars are often covered with circles of plain or checked cotton gingham held on with elastic bands. If the circles of gingham are cut with pinking scissors there is no need to stitch them. This looks very fresh and appetizing.

Make a marinade of 4 tablespoons of white wine and 4 tablespoons of brandy, with salt, pepper, ½ teaspoon of allspice, 3 crushed juniper berries, a bay leaf and a sprig of thyme. In this marinate 225 g (8 oz) pig's liver and 225 g (8 oz) of chicken livers, both coarsely chopped, for about 24 hours.

Melt 225 g (8 oz) lard. Drain the chopped liver, reserving the marinade, and fry it gently in the lard, turning it to cook slowly all over. Stir a little of the strained marinade into the pan juices, scraping the bottom of the pan with a spoon so all the delicious bits clinging to it are incorporated in the mixture. Then put all the ingredients in the electric blender and make a soft velvety purée, adding a little more of the marinade if necessary.

Danish Leverpostej*

This Danish liver pâté is almost a national dish. It has a light fluffy texture and is usually turned out on a dish to slice in portions, for the Scandinavian Cold Table or to make smørrebrød.

Put 1 medium-sized onion, previously peeled and chopped, and 900 g (2 lb) of sliced pig's liver through the fine plates of the mincer. Then put 450 g (1 lb) of fat bacon, without the rind and cut in chunks, through the mincer twice. Melt 50 g (2 oz) of butter, stir in 2 tablespoons of flour, and then, gradually, stir in 450 ml (¾ pint) of single cream, heating and stirring until you have a smooth, very thick sauce. Add the minced bacon and heat, stirring, until it has melted into it. Then remove the pan from the heat and add the minced liver and onion. Add 2 teaspoons of salt, 1 teaspoon of pepper, a good pinch of ground ginger or ground cloves and 3 teaspoons of anchovy paste. Mix thoroughly, adding 2 beaten eggs.

Line a big 2 litre (2 quart) baking dish or about three 675 g (1½ lb) loaf tins, or suitable terrines, with rashers of bacon cut thin and stretched slightly with the blade of a knife. Add

23

the pâté mixture. Cover it with a double thickness of foil. Put the tins or terrines in a baking tin or other suitable vessel with enough warm water to come halfway up the sides of the dishes. Bake them in a moderately slow oven, 170°C (325°F)/Gas 3, until a knife blade or skewer thrust into the pâté comes out clean. If you are using the big baking dish, it will take 1½-2 hours, but the exact time depends on the size, shape and also thickness of the tins or terrines. Chill before serving, and turn out to serve.

Smoked Mackerel Paste*

This goes very well with a chilled white wine, which need not necessarily be expensive.

Put a smoked mackerel in hot water for about 1 minute before skinning and boning it and taking off the head. Mash the flesh with 50 g (2 oz) butter, the grated rind and juice of 1 lemon and a dash of Tabasco. Chill before serving with hot toast.

Paprikáspastétom

This is a scarlet pâté which can be turned out to serve. It comes from Budapest and it is delicious with rye bread, particularly the kind with caraway seeds in it.

Peel and dice an onion finely, heat 50 g (2 oz) of lard in a large frying pan and cook the onion gently till soft and golden. Stir in a dessertspoon of sweet paprika pepper and add 675 g (1½ lb) pie veal, diced and trimmed. Roll it in the melted lard and paprika. Add ½ teaspoon of salt and a couple of tablespoons of water, then put a lid on the pan and let it simmer gently, stirring from time to time and adding a very little water occasionally. There should never be a lot of liquid.

After 30 minutes stir in 1 tablespoon of tomato purée. When the meat is tender, let it cool and put the whole thing, meat and gravy, through the mincer, fine plates. Then, having beaten 6 egg yolks and 100 g (4 oz) of softened butter together till smooth and creamy, mix this roughly with the cold minced meat. Pack it into a suitable terrine.

24

Pâté for a Party*

Make some forcemeat by mixing 225 g (8 oz) of minced veal with 225 g (8 oz) of unsmoked minced streaky bacon (without the rind) and 450 g (1 lb) of minced pig's liver. Add 225 g (8 oz) of stale white breadcrumbs soaked in cold milk and squeezed out, 25 g (1 oz) of salt, some freshly ground black pepper, a little Cayenne pepper, thyme, rosemary and a very little finely chopped garlic. Mix well and stir in 3 whole raw eggs and a wineglass of brandy.

Line a fireproof dish with thin rindless rashers of bacon. Fill it with the forcemeat, cover the top with a piece of fat bacon, and on top of this lay a bay leaf and a sprig of thyme. Cover with foil and a lid. Stand the dish in a tin with enough hot water to come halfway up the sides and bake it in a moderate oven, 180°C (350°F)/Gas 4 for about 1¼ hours. Remove the lid and let it cool with a weight on top.

This is a recipe given to me some years ago by Madame Odette Pol Roger, head of the great champagne firm. It is a well-flavoured but relatively inexpensive pâté, most useful for a cold buffet party when flanked by salads and other things. In Reims they also serve champagne and large bowls of quails' eggs.

Pigeon and Walnut Pâté

This is a coarse-cut pâté which is made in the old-fashioned kitchen mincer; the electric blender gives it too smooth and fine a texture.

Take two plump pigeons. Stuff each one with a lump of butter mixed with salt, pepper and a very little Cayenne pepper. Then brown the birds in a small saucepan with plenty of frothing butter. Do them gently and turn them over and over until all sides are brown. Add a chopped bacon rasher if you wish. Now put them in a casserole or old-fashioned stew jar, adding the bacon and giblets, if any, and all the butter, juices, etc. from the pan. Add only 1 tablespoon of water. Cover the top tightly with foil and a lid and cook the pigeons for 2 hours in a moderate oven, 180°C (350°F)/Gas 4. Take the flesh off the bones, weigh it, add half its weight in shelled walnuts, and put the meat and nuts through the mincer. Mix it with about 50 g (2 oz) of softened butter, and add a tablespoon of sherry or brandy and a little more salt and pepper if necessary. Pack into a suitable terrine, and chill.

Rillettes*

This is a speciality of Touraine and Anjou. In the city of Tours and other towns in the Loire valley *rillettes* are sold in the markets and at pork butchers' shops. They are packed in little pots and sealed with lard, to eat well chilled, with crusty bread and perhaps a bottle of red wine.

They are made with half a pig's head. This is a most useful dish to prepare and freeze if one has bought half a pig for the freezer and this has included the half head. Alternatively, buy half an unsalted pig's head from the butcher. Get him to prepare it, and cut it in chunks which will fit into a large casserole. Add a sliced onion, some mixed herbs tied together with a piece of cotton to facilitate their removal later, salt, pepper and a very little water—only 1½ tumblers to 2.2 kg (5 lb) of meat and bone. It should not be wet. The result must be a fat paste and not a jelly.

Put a lid on the casserole and leave it all night, 6 or 7 hours in the slowest oven, 130°C (250°F)/Gas ½. Stir it before you go to bed. Next morning it should be cooked to a pulp with the meat dropping off the bones. Remove these, then mash and shred the meat with two forks. Do not use the electric mixer, as it makes the mixture too smooth. You should end up with about 900 g (2 lb) of meat and fat. Pack the meat pastes in little pots, seal them with their own lard, cover them with foil and chill.

Rillettes d'Oie et de Porc
(Rillettes de Tours)

Dice 450 g (1 lb) unsalted pork—half lean, half fat—and 450 g (1 lb) of breast of goose. Put it all in a pot with enough water to three-parts cover it. Add salt, pepper, 2 sage leaves and a *bouquet garni,* tied with cotton. Cook slowly and gently, covered, for 3 hours, until the meat is almost

26

dropping off the bones, and the water has evaporated almost completely. Pour it all into a large deep dish, removing the *bouquet garni*. Mash the rillettes thoroughly with a fork to break the meat into shreds. Let it cool and, when the mixture begins to go solid, stir it again thoroughly. Pack it in stoneware jars.

Rillettes Ménagère (Lapin et Porc)

Take two nice rabbits, bone them and dice the meat. Dice 1.8 kg (4 lb) lean pork tenderloin and 1.35 kg (3 lb) fat pork.

Pour a generous litre (2 pints) of water into a pot with ½ teaspoon salt per 450 g (1 lb) of meat, and stir till the salt melts. Then add first the fat pork, then the lean, and finally the rabbit. Let it cook over a moderate heat for 2½ hours, being careful to stop the chopped meat from sticking to the bottom of the pot. It's best to use an asbestos mat if you are cooking the meat on top of the stove. The pot can also be put in a moderate oven, 180°C (350°F)/Gas 2, for 2½ hours. Stir from time to time with a large wooden spoon, scraping the bottom well. (In France a large wooden paddle, perhaps from the laundry, is used.) When it is almost cooked, stir constantly, and when the pieces of meat are sufficiently done to be crushed with a fork, mash them lightly. When they begin to brown take the pot off the heat and pour in a glass of white wine at once. Cover the pot with a cloth, let it stand a few minutes and then put the rillettes into stoneware jars. They will keep for several months.

Rillettes de la Mer au Citron

This is a delicious pâté that I tasted at the famous restaurant La Reserve, at l'Alouette, 8 kilometres outside Bordeaux. M. Garcia, the *chef de cuisine*, was good enough to give me the recipe for it later.

Rillettes were originally a simple farmhouse speciality associated with the Loire valley but they have become so popular all over France that, as will be seen, a fashionable restaurant may have its own delicate, highly original version far removed from the traditional one. Tomato ketchup, used in this recipe, is now considered very chic in France.

Put 900 g (2 lb) of whiting fillets, without the skin and bones, into the liquidiser. Add 3 eggs, a little salt, and some white pepper. When you have reduced the fish to a smooth paste add 1 litre (1¾ pints) of cream and continue to blend it for 1 minute.

Butter a terrine, fill it with the purée, and cover the top with foil. Stand it in a water bath and bake it 40 minutes in a moderate oven, 180°C (350°F)/Gas 4. When cooked and cool, put it in the refrigerator and leave it overnight. Next day beat up the pâté in a basin with the aid of a fork. Add the grated rind of 2 lemons and the juice of one. Mix well. Add 175 g (6 oz) of smoked salmon, cut in fine strips, 3 tablespoons of tomato ketchup and 600 ml (1 pint) of mayonnaise.

Mix the whole thing well and arrange it in your terrines. To serve, put a tablespoon of it on each plate, with some hot toast.

'Russian' Game Pâté

Really a Danish recipe, this pâté often appears on the Scandinavian Cold Table, nestling in a bed of cracked ice. Coarse dark rye bread and chilled snaps or akvavit go well with it.

Make a purée with 450 g (1 lb) of boned roast game (hare, venison, ptarmigan, pheasant, etc.) and 100 g (4 oz) of butter. Add salt, pepper, 3 dessertspoons of grated cheese, 1 dessertspoon of Worcestershire sauce, and mix well. Then gradually add 100 g (4 oz) of melted butter and a small glass of red wine. Stir until light and fluffy. Chill.

Akvavit is served ice cold. At home the Danes chill it for several days in the fridge, but in restaurants it's brought to the table frozen in a solid block of ice. You can do this at home in the freezer with a large tin about 20 cm (8 in) deep and 7.5 cm (3 in) wider than the akvavit bottle. First freeze 2.5 cm (1 in) of water in the bottom of the tin, and then stand the bottle on it. Add cold water nearly to the top and freeze again. Before serving dip the tin quickly into a pan of hot water. The bottle will come out together with its ice block.

Sardine and Lemon Pâté*

Melt 50 g (2 oz) butter, remove from the heat and stir in 75 g (3 oz) white or brown breadcrumbs. Use natural bread-crumbs, whether fresh or from the freezer, but not the dyed ones sold in packets. Add a dessertspoon of finely chopped parsley, the juice and grated rind of half a lemon, and the contents of a 100 g (4 oz) can of sardines, boned and mashed with oil. Beat the whole thing till smooth, taste it and add any necessary salt and pepper. Pack it into about 6 little dishes or potting pots, or into a large terrine. Put sliced lemon or a bit of parsley on top, and chill until firm.

Those Danish lemon 'butterflies' look well on this pâté. Make a cut in a slice of lemon from one side through the centre and halfway to the opposite side; by twisting the ends in opposite directions the lemon slice can be made to stand up. Slices of cucumber can be treated in the same way.

This particular pâté may also be covered in foil, sealed in a polythene bag and frozen. Thaw it at room temperature for 3 hours and serve it, chilled, with hot toast and lemon wedges (these may also be frozen).

Cod's Roe Pâté*

Chop 225 g (8 oz) smoked cod's roe and blend it to a purée in the electric blender with 1 peeled, chopped garlic clove, the strained juice of 1 lemon, a little parsley and, if liked, a dash of Tabasco. Add oil to taste and serve with hot toast.

Taramosaláta*

Alan Davidson, in his invaluable *Mediterranean Seafood*, says that the dried roe of the grey mullet was apparently used at one time in Greece for making taramosaláta; nowadays they make it with imported smoked cod's roe instead as it is less expensive than the original ingredient. This is his recipe.

Mix together 450 g (1 lb) of smoked cod's roe, 350 g (12 oz) of cream cheese, 3 tablespoons of olive oil, and 3 tablespoons of finely chopped chives. Finally stir in 3 tablespoons of lemon juice. Mix well and chill. Taramosaláta keeps well.

La Tapenade*

A luscious black pâté, strong and earthy, this is popular in the Roussillon with freshly baked bread and thinly sliced *saucisson de ménage*.

Stone 275 g (10 oz) of black olives (usually cheaper and better bought loose from a delicatessen). Add 2 teaspoons of capers, a dash of brandy, a large peeled chopped garlic clove, 2 salt 'barrel' anchovies (from delicatessens) boned, rinsed and dried in a towel. Combine all this in the electric blender to make a purée, adding 2 or more tablespoons of olive oil to make a firm but easily workable paste. Store in little pots.

Wiener Huehnerleberpastete*
(Austrian Liver Pâté)

Fry 225 g (8 oz) of chicken livers and a small finely chopped onion gently in butter, adding salt, pepper, and a good pinch of paprika pepper. Beat 2 eggs with a little milk. Pour them into the frying pan with the livers and stir, then let the mixture set.

Put the liver and egg in an electric blender, adding 1 tablespoon of butter and a spoonful of wine, brandy or other spirits, and blend to a purée. Taste for seasoning. Form it into a brick shape, or put it in a terrine, and chill.

In Austria, filled sandwich loaves are popular for parties. The filling could be *Liptoi* (page 109) or chicken liver pâté. Take a long white Vienna loaf, cut off the ends, take out all the soft inside part and then fill it with the chilled chicken liver pâté. Wrap it in foil and freeze, or chill it in the refrigerator for some hours before slicing and serving it.

30

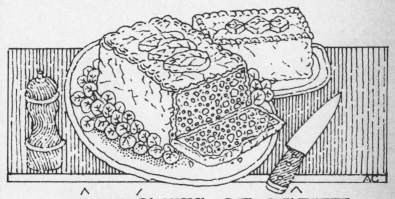

PÂTÉS EN CROÛTE

Almost any traditional pâté can be cooked *en croûte* provided it is not too wet, for that would make the pastry soggy. The *pâté de foie aux pruneaux* on page 17 is very good *en croûte*, and so is the *pâté de foie de porc ménagère* on page 21. Most pâtés were designed originally to be cooked in pastry, not in a dish. In the days before everyone had a domestic oven, people used to take them round to the baker to be cooked—hence the decorations on the pastry, which enabled the owner to recognize the pie when it was baked.

Though *pâté de foie gras* is mostly sold now in those pale pottery terrines with the lion's-head handles, or even in tins, it can still be had *en croûte* in the ancient manner, at very short notice and considerable expense flown especially from Strasburg; the magnum of champagne to go with it might seem a mere inexpensive detail in comparison. *Pâté de foie gras en croûte* is also available in London at Christmas, usually at Fortnum and Mason, Justerini and Brooks, or Jacksons.

There are other famous *pâtés en croûte*. Amiens is renowned for its duck pâté, traditionally made in a pastry crust though now more frequently prepared *en terrine*, but whether *en croûte* or *en terrine* it contains a whole boned stuffed duck. The *pâté en croûte* from the cathedral town of Chartres is another regional speciality. For this a fluted pie mould is lined with pastry, then filled with a rich forcemeat and laced with fillets of chicken, or sometimes pheasant marinated in port. The nearby town of Pithiviers is known for its lark pâtés, which are sent all over France. This is one of those things, like *pâté de foie gras*, that are virtually uncookable. Recipes vary slightly but usually tell one to bone from 40 to 60 larks completely, reserving the entrails and mashing these with a lump of *foie gras* and some truffles. The entrails are then used to stuff the birds, which are cooked in a rectangular pastry case with their heads and feet sticking through the crust. Quite apart from the horror of the whole idea, the lark is a protected bird in Britain and it is an offence to kill it or to offer it for sale; similarly protected here are the plovers, lapwings, blackbirds and thrushes sometimes made into pâtés elsewhere. It is perhaps no more cruel to kill a singing bird than a domestic chicken nor more wicked to murder a prima donna than an ordinary woman, but it seems wrong somehow.

The best *pâtés en croûte* are finished with a well flavoured jellying stock, made without added gelatine. (See chapter on aspic.) If this is the case the proud hostess might well say so. It is easily achieved by adding a split pig's foot, or possibly a dressed cowheel (calves' feet are virtually unobtainable now in Britain—either the beast runs on roller skates or they all go to the catering trade) to the bones, poultry carcase, giblets, etc., which are being simmered to make stock.

Carefully buttered hinged moulds, which may be round, oval, or rectangular, are used in France for *pâtés en croûte*. They are sold inexpensively by catering-trade suppliers in Britain, and the pies look charming, often with a sort of fluted wasp-waist in the middle. Some of these hinged moulds have a base. Others must stand on a baking sheet, but they all come apart when the metal pins are taken out at each end, so one can get the pie out without breaking it. They can be used for English hot-water crust pastry as well as *pâte à pâtés* and *pâte à foncer*.

The top of a French pie or *pâté en croûte* is usually decorated very simply—just marked with a herring-bone pattern with a sharp knife and brushed with an egg; sometimes pastry crescents and diamonds are added.

French Pie Pastry

Sometimes what is called *pâte à foncer* or *lining pastry* is used for *pâtés en croûte*. It is not very different from English shortcrust pastry, except that it is mixed not with water but an egg, and is similar to that used for lining flan rings and flan tins when making *quiche lorraine* or *tarte aux fruits*. The resulting pastry is very good.

Sift 225 g (8 oz) of plain flour into a basin. Add ½ teaspoon of salt, 60 g (2½ oz) butter and 40 g (1½ oz) lard

34

cut in pieces. Rub the ingredients lightly between the fingertips until it is sandy in texture. Add an egg, mixing it in with a fork, and then a very little very cold water if necessary to blend it into a compact mass of dough that does not separate. The inexperienced nearly always add too much water to pastry. Chill the pastry for an hour before rolling it out.

Pâte à pâté is the kind of pastry often used by *charcutiers* for *pâtés en croûte,* made straight on the pastry board. French cooks seldom use a bowl for making pastry. They heap the flour on a pastry board or marble-topped table, and make a well in the middle into which all the other ingredients are put. They then mix and knead it with their hands until they have a smooth dough free from cracks. But of course the same pastry can be made in a bowl if more convenient.

Heap 275 g (10 oz) plain sifted flour on to a pastry board and make a well in the middle. Put ¼ teaspoon salt, 75 g (3 oz) softened butter and 40 g (1½ oz) softened lard in it. Mix it all together, add 2 egg yolks and 3 tablespoons of cold water. Knead them all together. When the mixture is almost one, perfect it by patting it out with the palm of your hand. Flatten it on the pastry board with the palm of your right hand, pushing it towards you. Repeat this twice to make a well-mixed dough with enough body for a pastry that can hold a heavy filling. The meat and so forth often has a little liquid with it which might soften a very delicate pastry and make it soggy. When the dough is ready wrap it in a cloth and chill till wanted. It is best made some hours in advance. The pastry should be rather firm.

The pie

The various meats for the filling are often marinated in cognac or armagnac, Calvados or sometimes in port or Madeira. Almost any pâté or terrine mixture can be baked if liked in pastry instead of in a terrine.

Butter the metal pie mould carefully, making sure that all the hollows and indentations of the pattern have been buttered too.

Roll out the pastry, whether *pâte à foncer* (page 34) or *pâte à pâté* (above), about 1 cm (½ in) thick. Cut out a round or oval, according to the shape of the metal mould, which is big enough to line the bottom and sides with 2 cm (¾ in) to spare all round, to allow for shrinkage. Stand the mould on a metal baking sheet and line it with the pastry. Press this well into all the hollows. Trim the edge to make an even 1 cm (½ in) border. Damp the edge.

Now fill it with the chosen pâté mixture—but do not add any liquid as this would soften the pastry. Roll out the rest of the pastry to make a lid, slightly too large to allow for shrinkage. Moisten the edges with milk or water, using a pastry brush, and pinch them together to seal them. Make a small hole to let out the steam in baking, and put a small foil funnel in it, to keep it open. Make a pattern on top with a knife. Use any pastry left-overs to make simple trimmings if liked. Brush over with beaten egg.

Bake the pie in a moderately hot oven, 190°C (375°F)/Gas 5, for 3 hours. Cover the top lightly with foil if it is becoming too brown. When the pie is done let it cool for 45 minutes at the very least before removing the mould, otherwise it sags in the middle. Then brush the sides with egg, put a piece of foil on top and 'glaze' or brown it briefly in the oven.

When the pie has cooled for a couple of hours pour the jellying stock (page 98), if any, through the hole in the top, using a funnel.

Pâté de 'Foie Gras' Truffée de la Tante Louise

This is made after an old domestic recipe which has nothing whatever to do with the famous *pâté de foie gras*, in all honesty. All the same it is very good when baked *en croûte*.

Trim 450 g (1 lb) of poultry livers of any stringy or discoloured pieces. Cut them in 1 cm (½ in) chunks. Slice the contents of a small can of truffles as thinly as possible and save the liquor.

Chop 450 g (1 lb) of calf's liver (or pig's liver if need be), 100 g (4 oz) lean unsalted pork, and 225 g (8 oz) salted pork belly (or *petit salé*) without the rind or bones. Add 1 cup of fine soft white breadcrumbs, moistened with ¼ cup of water and squeezed out. Also add any truffle trimmings. Put

1 cm (½ in) of this coarse forcemeat on the bottom of the pastry-lined metal mould, then a layer of poultry livers and a single layer of sliced truffles. Repeat until the pastry is tightly packed, sprinkling a little salt and *les 4 épices* (page 129) lightly after each layer of very thinly sliced truffles.

Put on the pastry lid, decorate and trim the pastry crust. Bake the *pâté en croûte* as described on the previous page.

Add the truffle liquor to the jellying stock (page 98) which you will pour through the hole in the top of the pastry crust with the aid of a funnel, when the pâté has cooled.

If the *pâté de la Tante Louise* is baked *en terrine* instead of *en croûte*, put 1 cm (½ in) of forcemeat on the bottom of a greased terrine, then the poultry livers etc. until the terrine is almost full. Cover with a thin layer of pork fat and a bay leaf. Then cover the top of the terrine tighly with foil and a lid and bake it in a water bath in a slow oven, 150°C (300°F)/Gas 2, for about 3½ hours. Let it cool in the terrine, then chill. When thoroughly chilled the pâté may be unmoulded by plunging the dish in boiling water for a moment (not of course so far as to come into the pâté), then turning it upside down on a small platter. To be traditional, it should be wrapped and served in metal foil.

Pâté de Canard d'Amiens

Bone the duck as described on page 78 and lay it on the kitchen table skin side down. Slice off some of the thickest layer of leg and breast meat and chop this in 1 cm (½ in) cubes. Season them with salt, pepper, allspice, 2 tablespoons of Calvados or cognac and put them back in the duck, rolling it up and putting it in a bowl. Chill in the refrigerator for a couple of hours.

Make 900 g (2 lb) of pork and veal forcemeat (page 40) adding the pieces of diced duck and the marinade together with any meat from the duck carcase, the duck liver and heart, all finely chopped. Add 2 beaten eggs.

Now lay the boned duck once more, skin side down, on the kitchen table. Heap the stuffing in the middle in a sort of loaf shape, bring the duck skin up round it and sew this together (with a trussing needle and white string, or white button thread). Also tie some string round the duck at intervals, two or three times, to make it a sausage shape. Brown the duck lightly all over in 3 tablespoons of oil in a frying pan. Take it out and let it cool. Do not remove the trussing strings.

Having previously made and chilled 675 g (1½ lb) of *pâte à foncer* (page 34) roll about two-thirds of it into an oval 0.3 cm (⅛ in) thick. Lay it on a greased baking sheet and put the duck on it, breast up. Bring the pastry up round it, patting it in place. Roll the rest to make a 'lid' to fit over the top of the duck. Brush the edges of the pastry with egg yolk, press the 'lid' on and pinch the edges together. Use any remaining pastry for decoration. Brush the pie with beaten egg, make a small hole in the top and put in a little funnel made of rolled-up foil. Bake it in a moderate oven, 180°C (350°F)/Gas 4, for about 2 hours.

Let it cool thoroughly for several hours before putting it in the refrigerator, as the pastry softens if chilled too soon.

To serve the *pâté de canard d'Amiens* cut round the pastry crust, just under the join of the lid, before bringing it to table. Lift it off carefully in one piece. The duck will have shrunk away from the crust in cooking and can be lifted out. Do this, remove the trussing string, and also cut and pull out the sewing strings underneath. Put the duck back in the pastry and replace the pastry lid.

The carver slices the duck down like a sausage. This can be done either by slicing right down through the pastry crust, or by removing the duck from its pastry case and slicing it separately.

Pâté en Croûte Roskilde

This is a delicious recipe from Marethe Kjøller Hansen of the Meat Research Institute in Roskilde, Denmark, where it has been devised on your behalf. It is very good, neither very expensive nor difficult to make.

For the pastry sift 350 g (12 oz) of flour and a teaspoon of salt. Rub in 175 g (6 oz) of butter until the mixture is like fine crumbs, then stir in enough cold water to make a smooth dough. Chill the dough in the refrigerator for 24 hours before use.

Slice about 350 g (12 oz) of pork tenderloin, or fillet, in rounds and marinate it for some hours or overnight in 150 ml (¼ pint) of Madeira or sherry, mixed with a little chopped sage and thyme.

For the forcemeat, mince 350 g (12 oz) of lean pork, 225 g (8 oz) of lean veal, 225 g (8 oz) of smoked bacon and 225 g (8 oz) of pig's liver. Stir in 2 large or 3 small eggs and the marinade from the tenderloin. Flavour the forcemeat with a little pepper, 1 teaspoon of powdered sage, 1 teaspoon of powdered thyme and finally about 2 tablespoons of cognac. The forcemeat should be rather firm.

Roll out two-thirds of the dough about 1 cm (½ in) thick and use to line a round greased cake tin about 20 cm (8 in) across and with a removable bottom. The dough should come 0.5 cm (¼ in) over the top. Cover the dough-lined base with a layer of forcemeat, using a little to line the sides as well. Over this put a layer of pieces of pork tenderloin. They should not quite touch. Put some stuffed olives between them. Then repeat, with another layer of forcemeat and more pieces of tenderloin, and finally a layer of forcemeat. The tin must only be filled to within 2.5 cm (1 in) of the top. Roll out the rest of the pastry to make a 'lid', preferably a bit wider than the tin. Lay it on the forcemeat, brushing the edges with a little beaten egg, egg white or cold milk. Brush the edges of the dough in the tin, too, and bend them over the lid and press them down. Cut two holes in the lid the size of a new penny. Roll some pieces of greaseproof paper to make small 'chimneys' and put one in each hole to allow the steam to escape during cooking. Place the *pâté en croûte* in a hot oven, 200°C (400°F)/Gas 6, and immediately reduce it to a moderate heat, 180°C (350°F)/Gas 4. Bake it at this temperature for 1¼-1½ hours. When the meat juice trickles out, the pâté is baked.

Let it cool for 20 minutes, then loosen the edges so you will be able to turn out the pâté when it is nearly cold. Serve with a mixed salad and a long French loaf.

Pâté de Chartres en Croûte

The great plain of La Beauce near Paris is one of the richest districts in France for feathered game. The birds feed on corn. In Chartres, the administrative capital, they make good pâtés from pheasants and partridges, some with added truffles and *foie gras*. Some are cooked in round pastry cases, others in oval terrines sealed with lard. They are always eaten cold. When game is lacking the *pâté de Chartres* is made from domestic chickens from the neighbouring *départements* of Sarthe and Mayenne.

Take all the meat off the bones of a raw chicken. Keep back enough of the best pieces to make two layers of fillets to put in the pastry case. Marinate these in 2 tablespoons of port. Make the forcemeat by mincing the rest of the chicken with 450 g (1 lb) of salted pork belly and 450 g (1 lb) of lean unsalted pork. Add freshly ground black pepper, *les 4 épices* (page 129) and just a little salt as some of the pork is salty. Finally stir in the chicken liver, roughly chopped, the juices from the marinade and 3 eggs beaten in 150 ml (5 fl oz) of cream.

Butter a hinged French pâté mould. Line it with well-chilled, rolled *pâte à foncer*, or lining pastry (page 34). There should be enough pastry to come up 2.5 cm (1 in) above the rim of the mould. Lay 2 thin rindless rashers of bacon across the bottom, and cover this with half the forcemeat. Add half the marinated chicken fillets, then the rest of the minced mixture with the remaining fillets. Finish with a bacon rasher. Put on a 'lid' of pastry, moisten the edges and crimp them together with your fingers. Cut a small hole in the lid and insert a little funnel made of rolled-up foil. Bake the *pâté en croûte* in a moderate oven, 180°C (350°F)/Gas 4, for 2½ hours.

La Tourte Bourguignonne

A traditional delicacy once served at the amazing country weddings in *la basse Bourgogne*, which are said, in earlier times, to have continued for several days of feasting and drinking. It could be eaten hot or cold.

Chill about 675 g (1½ lb) of *pâte à foncer* (page 34) for several hours. Dice 450 g (1 lb) of lean veal (or use pie veal, which is sold diced) and 450 g (1 lb) unsalted pork fat. Mix the two and add salt, pepper, 2 large peeled crushed garlic cloves, 1 peeled chopped onion, 1 tablespoon of chopped parsley, *les 4 épices* (page 129) and 4 tablespoons of cognac. The forcemeat should not be too fine and is always carefully hand chopped rather than minced.

Divide the pastry into 2 parts. Roll out one part about 1 cm (½ in) thick on a floured board, and use this to line a shallow greased ovenproof tin. Fill it with the forcemeat, rolled into balls the size of an egg, leaving a little space between them. Roll out the other piece of pastry to make a lid. Moisten the edges of this and of the pastry in the tin, lay the lid over the meat balls and pinch the edges together. Mark the top in squiggles, or in a herring-bone pattern with a fork. Brush with beaten egg. Cut a hole in the middle to let the steam out, and bake it in a moderate oven, 180°C (350°F)/Gas 4, for about 50 minutes.

Pâté en Croûte, Mimi Hugel

This is a recipe which was given to me some years ago by Mme Hugel of Riquewihr in Alsace, a French wine village which is almost unchanged since the sixteenth century. Her husband, M. Jean Hugel, has twelve generations of wine-making ancestors, and is head of the well-known wine firm. He often speaks with great feeling of the happy marriages of wine and food, of the local dishes which blend perfectly with his dry Muscat wine, with the Gewürztraminer and the pale dry Riesling which makes me feel as though I were drinking liquid pearls. When one meets his wife Mme Mimi Hugel, now in her seventies, one realizes how happy that marriage of wine and food can be. Like most women in this part of France she is a superb cook but she is also mistress of the ancient art of the coquetry of the kitchen, or seduction by saucepan. Her husband and three sons all love her for it.

In Alsace they specialize in all kinds of splendid *pâtés en croûte;* there are said to be forty-two different kinds made from pork, beef, venison, duck, chicken, goose, wild boar, pheasant, and the famous *foie gras,* as well as from fish and even (on special occasions) from peacocks. Typically, the pâtés are highly spiced, with pepper, ground cloves, cinnamon, nutmeg, and ginger as well as garlic and mustard.

41

Cut 675 g (1½ lb) of lean pork in fingers. Put these in a pickle or marinade of 2 glasses of dry white wine, 1 sliced onion, 12 peppercorns, 2 bay leaves, a little salt and 12 crushed juniper berries, and leave to marinate for 4 hours.

Make your shortcrust pastry with 225 g (8 oz) of flour, 100 g (4 oz) butter, and a pinch of salt. Add the yolk of an egg and a drop of water to mix. Chill it for 2 hours in the fridge before rolling it out in two long narrow strips.

Drain and wipe the meat and roll it in a little ground allspice, salt and pepper. Put a layer of chopped onion and parsley on one strip of pastry, then a layer of pork running lengthwise. Repeat till finished. Lay the other strip of pastry on top, tucking in the edges and wrapping them under so that the pie resembles a big roly-poly. Then for the real Hugel garnish make a pattern on top by pinching up scraps of pastry between two forks turned back to back. Bake the pâté for an hour in a pre-heated hot oven, 200°C (400° F)/Gas 6. Serve cold and sliced, garnished with clear chopped aspic jelly (page 98).

Pâté en Croûte, Façon d'Albert

This is a modern Parisian *pâté en croûte* very different from the old country specialities. It is made not only with packaged puff pastry but flavoured with a little tomato ketchup, which has become very fashionable in France. 'It is', my friend Danielle said recently, 'because we go to England on holiday, and have such nostalgia afterwards for London. Ketchup is almost the only thing you can take back in your suitcase which reminds you of English cooking. I have some, it is exquisite, have you tried it with le bacon-and-eggs?' I said I had.

The pâté is to be served cold, sliced, and with a green salad.

Roll out 450 g (1 lb) of packet puff pastry on a floured board, making a rectangle about 17.5 × 30 cm (7 × 12 in) and 1 cm (½ in) thick. Then make two smaller rectangles from the trimmings, each 20 × 10 cm (8 × 4 in). Lay one of these on the larger piece of pastry, in the middle so that the pastry case will be thicker at the bottom.

For the forcemeat or filling, mince 350 g (12 oz) of veal or chicken, mix it with a peeled crushed garlic clove, a little powdered thyme and powdered bay leaf, some salt and freshly ground black pepper. Add 225 g (8 oz) good coarse-cut pork sausagemeat, mix them well together, then fry the stuffing gently in a little oil and butter, stirring and mixing to cook it lightly. Add 1 tablespoon of French mustard and 1 tablespoon of tomato ketchup and an egg to bind.

Let the forcemeat become cold before arranging it, in two neat layers, on the smaller rectangle in the centre of the pastry. Bring up the edges of the pastry to enclose the meat and make a pastry case, moistening the edges slightly. Now put the other small rectangle on top as a lid, pinch the dampened edges together and brush the pastry with beaten egg. Bake it on a greased baking sheet in a hot oven, 200°C (400°F)/Gas 6, for about 30 minutes.

Raised pies

'The French', as Eliza Acton remarked in *Modern Cookery for Private Families, Reduced to a System of Easy Practice,* 1845, 'excel greatly in this form of pie . . . We remember having partaken of one which was brought from Bordeaux, and which contained a small boned ham of delicious flavour, surmounted by boned partridges, above which were placed fine larks likewise boned; all the interstices were filled with super-excellent forcemeat, and the whole, being a solid mass of nourishing viands, would have formed an admirable traveller's larder in itself.'

Hot Water Crust Pastry

Hot water crust pastry is the kind used for English raised pies. This is one of the oldest forms of pastry going back at least to the Middle Ages when a pie was known as a *coffyn* or *coffer,* a little box or enclosure for something precious such as meat. In France a slightly different pastry is used containing egg yolks and it is not raised by hand.

Lard is the most usual fat for hot water crust pastry but butter could be used instead and nowadays some cooks use corn oil. Unlike other pastries this one is mixed with warm liquid. It must be done quickly so the pastry is warm, and yet not too hot, so that it is easy to mould or raise it in the shape of a pie. If it is too cold it will be difficult to mould it without breaking it; if it is too hot it will be soft and floppy and may collapse.

Sift 450 g (1 lb) of plain flour into a basin with a pinch of salt. Make a well in the middle. Heat 150 g (5 oz) of lard in a pan with 150 ml (¼ pint) of water. Bring to the boil and take it off the heat. Pour all this into the flour and mix it up quickly in a warm place, kneading it gently, then let it stand in a warm place for 30 minutes to recover. Now roll it out lightly on a lightly floured pastry board and mould or raise it in the shape of a pie. This is not very difficult to do round a 1 kg (2 lb) oiled or floured jam jar. If a larger pie is to be made use a floured tin, such as a round biscuit tin. When the pastry is up to the edge, roll the jar sideways to smooth the outside and loosen the pastry. Trim the top of the paste with scissors and leave it to set before removing the tin or jam jar. A piece of dough should have been kept back for the pastry 'lid' and for the pastry leaves and roses.

If the pie is to be raised entirely by hand it is best to begin with very small ones which are easier to manage. Mould the pastry while still warm. Divide the dough into two pieces—one using about a quarter of the dough which is for the lid and should be put in a warm place with a cloth over it while the bigger piece is being moulded. Hollow the bigger piece out into a round with your knuckles and draw the sides up to form a case, say about 10 cm (4 in) across and about 0.5 cm (¼ in) thick, trimming the edges with scissors if necessary. It is best to get someone, such as the local baker or pork butcher, to show you how to do this. But it is by no means difficult, and very gratifying when done.

Decorations for Raised pies

Rose leaves are made by cutting small diamond shapes from scraps of pastry. Then, with the point of a knife, they are marked with a long central line with other lines coming off at an angle, to represent the veins of a leaf. Moisten the backs, curl them slightly and stick them on the pastry 'lid' around the opening.

44

Roses are made by cutting strips of pastry about 0.5 cm (¼ in) deep and perhaps 7.5-10 cm (3-4 in) long, then rolling them up. As they are rolled the pastry is pulled out into little peaks to make petals. This is easier to do than to describe. Moisten the bases of the roses and stick them between the leaves around the opening in the pie crust. Smaller roses are made in the same way.

Acorns can easily be made from little balls of pastry. One end should be damped, then a small strip of pastry is wrapped round the end and marked with a fork, to look like the acorn cup.

Oak leaves are made like rose leaves but cut with a wiggly outline.

None of this is at all difficult, though perhaps rather fiddly. The thing is that the leaves and flowers—if one may say so—do not have to be very good. The eye makes up for any discrepancies and people take a childish delight in them.

Pork Pie (Midlands recipe)

Make the hot water crust pastry (page 43), using 450 g (1 lb) of flour and kneading it on a floured board till smooth. Cut off a quarter of the dough and put it aside covered with a warm cloth. Mould the rest, as fast as you can, into a high pie case. Or if you like put a 1 kg (2 lb) jam jar in the middle of the pastry and mould it round that. It is important to work very quickly when using hot water pastry and also to keep it warm while moulding it. The hot dough is flexible, but it hardens as it cools and then cannot be moulded at all. Fasten one or two layers of greaseproof paper round the outside of the moulded pie—in a sort of collar—so it doesn't sag in the middle before hardening in the oven.

Fill the pie quickly with the meat, packing it tight. Allow nearly 675 g (1½ lb) pork, wipe it with a damp cloth, trim off any gristle, and cut it very small using a good kitchen knife held straight in both hands. Do not mince it or blend it to a purée. There should be two parts lean pork to one part fat pork, well mixed with a little salt and a dash of anchovy essence stirred very well into it. Moisten with a very little stock.

45

Roll out a circle of pastry to make the lid. Place it on the pie and pinch the edges together. Make a hole in the centre of the pie, then decorate with pastry leaves and roses and brush with beaten egg. Put it on a greased baking sheet. Bake it in a hot oven, 200°C (400°F)/Gas 6, until the top is golden brown, then reduce the heat to moderate, 180°C (350°F)/Gas 4, and bake for 2 hours, covering the top with a piece of foil or greaseproof paper if it is getting too brown. After 1 hour take the pie from the oven on its baking sheet, take the paper off the sides, brush them with egg, and put the pie back to finish cooking.

The jelly which is poured into the pie through the hole in the top (with the aid of a funnel) when the pie is baked is made by stewing any pork gristle and oddments with a pig's foot. It should be made first, started the night before perhaps. Put the split unsalted pig's foot and pieces of pork, gristle etc. in a pan with 6 peppercorns, 1 medium-sized carrot trimmed and sliced, and 1 onion stuck with 4 cloves. No salt, and water just to cover. Pressure cook for 40 minutes, and strain into a clean pan.

The pie is usually eaten cold but can be eaten hot. When made rather larger it makes a good family pie, for a lot of people for Christmas. The quantities of everything should be increased.

Veal and Ham Pie

This is a popular old favourite which because of the shortage of veal is usually made now with chicken or turkey. It can be very dull if not well flavoured.

Pour boiling water over 225 g (8 oz) raw gammon, forehock or bacon pieces, then dice it. Chop 550 g (1¼ lb) boneless pie veal fairly small. Season well with ¼ teaspoon allspice, a little pepper, some chopped parsley, fresh thyme and the grated rind of 1 lemon. Mix well, add 2 whole shelled hard-boiled eggs, or 2 whole well drained pickled walnuts. Moisten with stock.

Pack all this into the raised pie crust (page 43) and bake it as before. Fill with jellying stock made from veal and ham trimmings and 1 split pig's foot (see Pork Pie).

Raised Rabbit Pie

Mince 225 g (8 oz) pork—half fat, half lean—and mix it with ½ teaspoon freshly ground nutmeg, ½ teaspoon ground cloves, and ½ teaspoon freshly ground black pepper.

Bone a small rabbit—there should be about 450 g (1 lb) of meat when done—cut most of it into neat fillets and mince any oddments with the pork. Marinate the rabbit fillets in brown sherry for 12 hours, with a little salt, 12 peppercorns, and 1 peeled minced onion. Wipe the fillets dry. Add the marinade to the rabbit bones and a pig's foot and boil these down in the pressure cooker to make stock which will be poured into the pie when cooked.

Fill the raised pie with the pork and rabbit, put on a lid and bake it as before (see Pork Pie).

Scots Mutton Pies

This is a regional speciality. Almost all Scottish people like mutton pies, but they are rarely seen in England. Most English people have never heard of them, and do not much care for them if they have. They are popular with the Royal family, however, often served at parties and receptions at Buckingham Palace as well as Balmoral, and still made for Queen Elizabeth II to the same recipe as that used in Queen Victoria's day.

The Great Mutton Pie Treat still takes place at Christmas in the Royal and Ancient Borough of Lauder (pop. 564) on the Scottish border, as it has for over a hundred years. The pies are given to children and old-age pensioners. The tradition started when in 1873 Mrs McDougall, a local farmer's wife, anxious that the village children were hungry at Christmas, had a sheep killed and made into pies which she used to give to poor children in the village. Her grandson still sends a sheep for the Treat to Mr Shaw, the local butcher, who is busy most of Christmas week cutting it up and preparing it for the pies which are made by Mr Angus Gilder in the bakehouse next door. He says they are 'a wee bit of an acquired taste. Very greasy you know, being pure minced mutton. But then you couldn't possibly buy a pure mutton pie anywhere in the shops in Britain now.'

'Piping hot, they're unbeatable,' says Archie Aitchison, landlord of the Black Bull, Lauder. 'The only trouble when we were children, and all dressed up for the occasion, was that the fat would run down on our best clothes. There used to be two Christmas trees in Lauder then, one for the boys and one for the girls. We ate the pies round them on Christmas Day itself.'

A hundred years ago the sheep were sent to the Manse to be cooked, probably because it was the only place with big kitchen skillets and fires to make a broth from the bones. 'I expect the meat was made into pies,' says the Reverend Richard James, 'because it was the fairest way of sharing out the gift equally.'

To make Scots mutton pies, add 100 g (4 oz) of best dripping and 1 teaspoon of salt to a pan containing 300 ml (½ pint) of boiling water. Pour this on to 450 g (1 lb) of plain flour and mix. When cool, form it into a lump and knead on a floured board.

Divide two-thirds of the dough into six to line small, straight-sided greased tins. After lining them with pastry, fill the tins with 350 g (12 oz) lean lamb or mutton chopped small. Add salt, pepper and freshly grated nutmeg and moisten with a little gravy. Make the rest of the pastry into lids. Damp the edge of the pastry, put the 'lids' on the pies and make a small hole in each lid. Brush them with milk to brown them in the oven. Bake the pies in a moderate oven, 180°C (350°F)/Gas 4, for 40 minutes. Fill up each pie, through the little hole, with gravy before serving.

Les Petits Pâtés de Pezénas

Mutton pies similar to those eaten in Scotland are also a speciality of the small town of Pezénas in the Pyrenees. This is because Clive of India, who died in 1774, went to Pezénas in France towards the end of his life to take a rest cure. He took a *château* near Larzac and entertained lavishly. Whether he had a Scots or an Indian cook is not known, but the little mutton pies were evidently very popular locally and seen as a sort of *pâté en croûte*.

A local *patissier*, Monsieur A. M. Roucairol, in the rue des

48

Chevaliers-Saint-Jean, managed to get the secret of how to make them and began making them for his customers. According to André Bonnaire in *La Cuisine Rustique du Languedoc* (Haute Provence 1971), 'Their reputation became universal, a reputation with sinister results for the little pâtés of Pezénas. Béziers, which is a more important town, usurped the recipe and gave its name to this *patisserie*, although modifying it slightly.' They are still much enjoyed locally.

For *les petits pâtés de Pezénas*, make a forcemeat of 225 g (8 oz) of lean roast mutton, 100 g (4 oz) of mutton kidney fat, the grated rind of 1 lemon, and 2 tablespoons of brown sugar.

Make a homogenous dough from 275 g (10 oz) of flour, 75 g (3 oz) of lard, a little salt and some water. Roll this out and make it into little round pots which you then fill with the forcemeat. Bake them in a hot oven, 200°C (400°F)/Gas 6, for 30 minutes. They are to be eaten hot.

For *les petits pâtés de Béziers*, fiercely competitive with the original version, make a *pâte brisée* with 275 g (10 oz) flour, 150 g (5 oz) of butter, a pinch of salt and rather less than 300 ml (½ pint) water. From this make the little pots as before and fill them with forcemeat and bake as before. In Béziers forcemeat is made by mixing 275 g (10 oz) minced mutton with 100 g (4 oz) minced mutton kidney fat, a handful of raisins and 2 tablespoons of brown sugar.

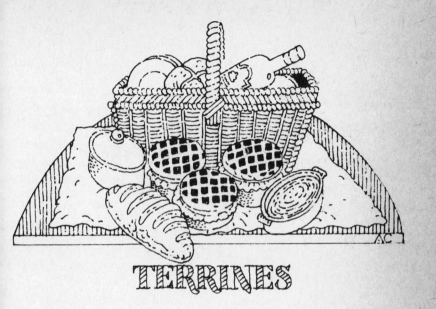

TERRINES

TERRINES ARE SIMPLY *pâtés en croûte* without the croûte, or pies without pastry. Prepared in this way they may be kept for much longer than when there is pastry.

Classically a terrine should be lined with bacon rashers or salt belly pork, or with a piece of *crépine* or veiling, before the pâté is put in. French terrines are covered in lard to seal them and keep out the air and preserve them from decay, whereas English ones are closed with clarified butter. If the terrine or pâté is being used, and has already been cut into, always put a piece of greaseproof paper or foil on the cut edge to keep out the air.

Terrines should be cooked in a water bath, or *bain marie*, in a hot oven. The water bath provides steam around the terrine and stops it drying. A roasting tin will do—the dish does not have to be deep. Enough water should be added, boiling, to come about halfway up the sides of the dish. Add more boiling water during cooking if necessary.

Old recipes tell one to seal the lid and hold it in place during cooking with a strip of flour and water paste or 'huff paste'—similar to that once used for baking a haunch of venison. This was popular about a hundred years ago but nowadays we use kitchen foil, more simply, for the same purpose.

Cook the terrine 30-35 minutes per 0.5 kg (1 lb). Then run a skewer or a steel knitting needle into it. This should come out burning hot, and the liquid around the meat will appear clear if the terrine is done, milky if it is not.

Now chill the whole thing, with a board or plate on top to fit inside the terrine. Put a weight on top, to press the meat together and make it compact when cold. Some cooks use the weights from the kitchen scales for this. Others balance a precarious arrangement of tins on top. The most practical way to weight a terrine, I think, is to stand a jug of water on top of the board, or plate, in the terrine. A jug is always to hand and the weight of water can be increased almost *ad infinitum*. All terrines are treated like this.

If you are adding jelly to pâtés and terrines, pour it in when they are quite cold. The jelly itself must be just melted, but cold. It is poured in only a few hours before serving. If jelly is to be added the fat should be taken off the terrine before it is chilled. When game is used, it is best to cook some game bones and carcases in the jelly for flavour.

Terrine (or tureen) of Hare

Use only part of the hare—the hind legs, liver and so on—for the terrine and jug the rest or make a pie of it.

Bone the meat, stripping off the fine membrane round it if possible. Put the pieces of hare in a marinade made from 150 ml (¼ pint) of white wine, 12 peppercorns, a bay leaf, a sprig of thyme, 2 tablespoons of whisky and a little salt. Leave it overnight.

Mix 450 g (1 lb) of minced pork with 50 g (2 oz) of minced streaky bacon, 1 tablespoon of chopped parsley and 1 small minced onion. Add a little pepper, 2 eggs and some of the marinade from the hare, and mix it well. Fill a well greased terrine with layers of the forcemeat, pieces of hare and some thin rashers of streaky bacon without the rind. Add a little more minced onion and the rest of the marinade. Cover the terrine closely with foil and a lid and stand it in a tin of enough hot water to come about halfway up the sides of the dish. Bake it in a slow oven, 150°C (300°F)/Gas 2, for about 3 hours. Let it cool, then cover it with a thin layer of melted lard to seal it from the air. Cover with foil and the lid. Chill.

Terrine of Fresh Salmon

A perfect summer dish which can be kept in the refrigerator for several days, though the accompanying mayonnaise should be made just before the pâté is to be eaten.

For the forcemeat, mix 100 g (4 oz) flour with 3 egg yolks and 150 ml (¼ pint) of milk in a pan off the heat, adding salt, some freshly milled black pepper and a pinch of nutmeg. Then heat it gently, whisking all the time until it thickens, but do not let it boil as the egg yolks would scramble. Take it off the heat immediately it thickens.

Add 3 dessertspoons of butter and 3 dessertspoons of shrimp butter. Blend them into the mixture with a spatula, letting it solidify over a very, very gentle heat for no more than 2-3 minutes. Let it cool for 30 minutes.

Now add one whole egg, 40 g (1½ oz) of chopped pistachio nuts, 2 tablespoons of brandy and 2 tablespoons of white wine. 25 g (1 oz) of chopped truffles should also be added if available. Then, having finely chopped 350 g (12 oz) white fish fillet, freed it of any skin and bone, and minced it, add this to the mixture, standing the bowl on ice for 10 minutes while you work it with a spatula to a perfectly smooth paste.

Cut 675 g (1½ lb) of fresh salmon in tiny fillets and season them with salt and pepper. Line a terrine (or rectangular pâté tin) with foil and cover it with a layer of salmon fillets, then one of forcemeat, then one of salmon fillets and so on until the dish is full. Cover with greaseproof paper and with foil, and pierce both layers of paper in two places with a steel knitting needle or fine steel skewer. Prod it right through to the bottom of the terrine. Stand the dish in a *bain marie* and bake it in a very moderate or moderate oven, 170-180°C (325-350°F)/Gas 3-4, for about 1¼ hours. Take it out of the oven, let it cool, and then chill for some hours.

To make shrimp butter, grind about 75 g (3 oz) of cooked shrimps in their shells to a purée with an equal weight of butter, a little lemon juice and enough paprika powder to make it a cheerful pink.

Terrine de Foie de Volaille au Poivres Noirs

A very pale, pinkish pâté in a brown earthenware pot with whole black peppercorns laid thickly on top. The peppercorns are not to be ground, but just crushed roughly with a kitchen weight, rolling pin or clock weight. The terrine is then covered with foil and left for 2 or 3 hours, then cooked in the oven. The aroma and flavour of the peppercorns will penetrate the contents of the terrine—I wouldn't eat them!

The terrine is often finished when cold with a thin layer of aspic which is poured on when almost setting.

Peel and chop 2 fat garlic cloves. Trim 450 g (1 lb) of chicken livers, removing any discoloured or stringy bits. Marinate them in 2 tablespoons of cognac for a couple of hours with a little tarragon and the chopped garlic. Then put them to soak in milk overnight in the refrigerator to make them a pale colour.

Next day, blend the chicken livers in the liquidiser with nutmeg and salt. Add 300 ml (½ pint) of double cream. Pack the mixture into a buttered terrine and top with the layer of crushed black peppercorns. Cover with foil and after 2 hours bake the terrine in a water bath in a moderate oven, 180°C (350°F)/Gas 4, for 1½ hours.

The water should just simmer gently; check it halfway through the cooking time and if necessary add some boiling water. Take out the terrine when done, wipe the pot and cool it for 2-3 hours on a rack, then chill in the fridge. Don't eat it for two days. It keeps a week in the fridge.

Terrine d'Anguilles au Vert à la Brabançonne

To make this famous Belgian dish, skin, gut and wash 900 g (2 lb) of eels. Cut them in slices, just stiffen them in 100 g (4 oz) butter and while they are cooking cover them with a good layer of fresh, green, well-washed sorrel, spinach, chervil, parsley, sage and winter savory all finely chopped and with nothing added except the water clinging to them. Let this mixture 'melt' for 5 minutes over a fairly low heat, with a lid on the pan. Then add 300 ml (½ pint) of light ale or white wine with enough water to cover. Season. Bring to the boil and cook briskly for 20-25 minutes.

Mix 3 egg yolks with the strained juice of 1 lemon and ½ teaspoon of cornflour in a basin. Add a little of the eel stock and stir. Add more, then add the egg mixture to the eel broth. Heat, stirring to thicken but without letting it boil, as the eggs will curdle.

Arrange the pieces of eel in a terrine and pour the thickened broth over. Serve cold.

56

Terrine de Lapin Grand'mère*

This makes a delicious simple meal with a green salad.

Line the terrine with thin rashers of salted pork belly or of green bacon, sliced very thin and without the rind. Put a 1 cm (½ in) layer of good farmhouse sausagemeat in the bottom of the terrine.

Cut up and bone a rabbit, cutting the meat in fingers and rolling it in a little freshly grated nutmeg, ground cloves, salt and pepper. Mix them with fingers of unsalted lean and fat pork, about the same weight, and the chopped rabbit liver.

Put a layer of peeled, thinly sliced carrot and onion on top of the sausagemeat, then one of the mixed rabbit and pork, then another layer of sausagemeat. Do not press down the layers. Continue until the terrine is almost full. Pour in white wine gently and slowly, almost to the top of the terrine. Cover with foil and a lid. Bake it for about 2 hours in a moderately slow oven, 170°C (325°F)/Gas 3. Cool for about 24 hours before serving.

This can be served straight from the terrine or turned out on a dish and cut in wedges. Hot, freshly baked baps would be good with it.

Terrine du Chef (Terrine Maison)

A recipe given to me by M. Claude Lablanche, distinguished *charcutier* of the rue Royale in Calais, and *meilleur ouvrier de France*. M. Lablanche explained that although their name for it is now a very common one, used and even abused by all sorts of people, the terrine is one of their specialities, and it is what they have always called it. The recipe has been handed down from father to son and may well go back to the origins of their establishment, in Soissons, in 1791.

It is a classic and very delicious *terrine du charcutier*, pink and luscious and not very expensive. It would be very nice for a cold buffet or to have on hand during a summer holiday. The quantities given below will of course make several terrines and be enough for 20-25 people, but they can be halved for a smaller party. The terrines will keep for a week or longer in a cool place, and should anyway be left for several days to mature.

Take 900 g (2 lb) of pig's liver, and 2 kg (4 lb) of unsalted neck of pork. In England this is generally sold as part of the hand and spring. It is seldom cut separately. If it is unobtainable unsalted pork belly could be used instead. Chop the meat roughly and mix it with 50 g (2 oz) cooking salt, about 15 g (½ oz) sugar and 1 small teaspoon of saltpetre. Leave to stand for 24 hours, so that the meat will be a rosy pink when cooked.

Now make a very fine forcemeat or purée with 100 g (4 oz) peeled chopped onion, 25 g (1 oz) peeled chopped shallot and 100 g (4 oz) of the meat, using the electric blender for this if liked.

Put the rest of the meat through the kitchen mincer with the coarse 0.5 cm (¼ in) plate on it. Mix both mince and purée together, adding 7 g (¼ oz) white pepper, half a teaspoon of ground allspice or *les 4 épices* (page 129), a little freshly grated nutmeg, a good dessertspoon of orange flower water (in bottles from good chemists) and 2 tablespoons of armagnac. Mix it all thoroughly together with your hands, gradually working in 5 medium eggs and 300 ml (½ pint) of tepid milk.

Line the terrines with *bardes* or strips of pork fat, then fill them with the mixture, packing it down carefully so there are no air pockets. Cover the tops with pieces of *crépine* or pig's caul (page 113) and garnish them with a sprig of thyme and a bay leaf. Put on a well fitting lid and a piece of foil tied down with string.

The cooking is done in two stages. Put the terrines first in a hot oven, 200°C (400°F)/Gas 6, until a fine golden crust is formed. Then reduce the heat to slow, 150°C (300°F)/Gas 2, to finish the cooking. A terrine of about 1 kg (2 lb) will take about 2 hours. It may be tested to see if it is cooked, as M. Lablanche explained, by thrusting the fine blade of a small knife into the middle of the pâté or terrine. Pull it out after a few seconds and lay it quickly on the back of your hand. If there is a slight burning sensation, the terrine is cooked, but if the knife blade is only tepid the terrine must be put back in the oven to go on cooking until it reaches the right temperature.

Weight the terrines and let them cool in a larder or some-where similar. Sprinkle them from time to time with *fond de veau* or *jus de couenne*—either a good well-reduced veal stock or one of those rich meat glazes or *jus* of which French chefs are so fond—made in this instance from lean pork trimmings, bones, pigs' feet, herbs and seasoning.

Terrine à la Birgit

This coarse-cut terrine is flavoured with dry vermouth and laced with stuffed olives and is a great success at Birgit's parties in Copenhagen. Birgit Wolstrup, who, with her husband Bent, has one of the finest collections of treen in Denmark, serves this dish cut in slices and accompanied by French bread sticks, extra olives and gherkins.

She says it is best sliced while still chilled from the refrigerator and that she always makes it in a metal mould to turn out. If a pretty terrine is used it tends to be left in it and dug at with a spoon, which spoils the flavour.

Put 550 g (1¼ lb) of chopped pig's liver and 450 g (1 lb) of medium fat chopped streaky pork through the mincer. Take a piece of pork tenderloin weighing about 275 g (10 oz), trim it, and cut it in long strips about 1 cm (½ in) wide. Add 4 peeled and grated shallots and 2 pressed garlic cloves to the minced meat and stir in 1½ level dessertspoons of salt, ½ teaspoon of freshly ground peppercorns, and 2 teaspoons of dried marjoram. Mix well and add 3 eggs and 150 ml (¼ pint) of dry vermouth, while stirring.

Take two metal moulds (of nearly 1 kg (2 lb) each) and fill them with layers of the minced meat, 175 g (6 oz) green olives stuffed with pimento, and the strips of pork tenderloin. The last layer must be minced meat. Cover the tops of the moulds with kitchen foil and place them in a pre-heated moderate oven, 180°C (350°F)/Gas 4, for 1½ hours.

After the moulds have cooled out of the oven for 15 minutes, press them under weights until completely cold.

This is enough for twelve people, and it freezes well for up to three months.

La Terrine Berrichonne

This is a regional delicacy made on farms and by *charcutiers* near Bourges, a district noted for the earthenware cooking

59

pots—*marmites, terrines,* and *gratin* dishes with a golden toffee-coloured glaze—which are sold in open-air markets all over France.

Marinate a nice wild rabbit for 24 hours in a covered dish and a marinade made from 2 tablespoons of olive oil, an onion sliced in rounds, some sprigs of thyme, a bay leaf, 300 ml (½ pint) of dry white wine and 3 tablespoons of *marc* (a local brandy or *eau-de-vie* made from fermenting grape skins, pips and stalks after the wine pressing). Add salt, pepper and some freshly grated nutmeg.

Make the forcemeat (*farce*) the next day, by chopping the rabbit liver roughly and mixing it with 175 g (6 oz) each of lean pork and unsalted fat pork coarsely minced. Mix it well, adding salt, pepper, nutmeg and a little *marc*. Stir in a beaten egg. Fry the forcemeat briefly in 50 g (2 oz) lard or bacon dripping. Wipe the rabbit, chop it almost in two across the back and fry it lightly in the lard or bacon dripping.

Blanch some pieces of pork fat or bacon rashers and line a casserole with them. Stuff the two parts of the rabbit with the forcemeat and tuck the rabbit around it. Put the animal in the casserole. Add a knuckle of veal and the strained marinade. Cover the pot closely with foil and a lid. Cook it in a very moderate oven, 170°C (325°F)/Gas 3, for 2 hours or until tender.

Bone the rabbit and the veal. Line a terrine with layers of rabbit, veal and forcemeat until it is almost full; the last layer should be rabbit. Skim the fat off the liquor in which the rabbit was cooked and strain it through a sieve into the terrine. Cover the terrine with a board or plate, put a weight on top and chill it until the next day.

This quantity is enough for about eight to ten people, depending on appetite. A local dry flinty white wine, Reuilly or Quincy, is mostly drunk with it.

Simple Terrine of Duck with Orange

It must be allowed time to mellow and ripen like wine. After it is weighted and cold it should be left several days in a cold larder or refrigerator for the flavours to develop before it is eaten.

Line the terrine with bacon rashers, sliced thin and with the rinds cut off, then stretched still thinner with the back of a knife. Take all the meat off the carcase of 1 duck, cutting most of the breast meat into neat strips which will be left whole.

Mince all the duck meat except the strips of breast, adding 6 coriander seeds, salt, a teaspoon of allspice, a pig's kidney, the duck liver, and lastly 2 tablespoons of breadcrumbs. I put these in last as they also serve to clean the mincer of any lingering bits of duck. Stir in an egg, salt and pepper.

Put a layer of this minced forcemeat—or *farce*—in the bottom of the bacon-lined terrine. Lay strips of breast meat on top, then more forcemeat and so on until the terrine is almost full. Add 2 tablespoons of Cointreau.

Cover the terrine with foil and a lid and place it in a water bath, or *bain marie*, a roasting or baking tin with hot water in it to come halfway up the terrine. Cook it in a moderate oven, 180°C (350°F)/Gas 4, for about 2 hours, filling up the roasting tin with more very hot water when necessary.

Thrust a skewer into the thickest part of the terrine to see if it is cooked. The juices should run perfectly clear (without a trace of blood) and the liquid fat surrounding the pâté should be quite transparent with no red juices. The pâté will have shrunk considerably and be bathed in melted fat and juice.

After the terrine is cold, it is best to weight it. This makes it firmer and easier to slice and presses out any air bubbles. Cover the top with several thicknesses of foil or greaseproof paper and then put a plate or a board on it which fits neatly inside the terrine, and put weights on this.

Remove all fat and juices when cold. Decorate the top with 2-3 bay leaves, some orange segments, and a few coriander seeds. Melt 15 g (½ oz) of gelatine in 2 tablespoons of orange juice, heating, stirring and adding 1 bouillon cube melted in 300 ml (½ pint) of hot water. Also add the juice from the pâté (without any of the fat at all). Let this cool, strain it over the pâté and chill.

Terrine de Canard

This recipe comes from a charming old Parisian restaurant, Au Roy Gourmet in the Place des Victoires. It opened in 1913 and with its frescoes and bentwood furniture has probably not changed since then. There is a fine equestrian statue of the 'Roy Gourmet'—Louis XIV—outside.

Take a 1 kg (2¼ lb) duck and remove the skin and bones. Chop the liver, heart and gizzard finely. Cut the duck meat in strips and put it in a large basin with salt and pepper and a *bouquet garni*. Pour some port over it to cover. Mince 450 g (1 lb) of pork and 550 g (1¼ lb) of shoulder of veal and add them to the duck. Let it all marinate together for 36 hours. Now take a terrine, put a layer of the duck fillets in the bottom, and then a layer of minced meats. Repeat this until the terrine is full, then cover the meat with a solid strip of pork fat. Put the terrine in a tin with hot water to come halfway up the sides of the dish. Bake in a moderate oven, 180°C (350°F)/Gas 4 for 2½ hours. Chill, and serve it in the terrine or turned out, if liked, on a long platter.

Terrine of Pork with Mushrooms

This inexpensive terrine comes from Budapest. It contains crisp bits of pork crackling, or what country people here call scruggins or pork scratchings, the little brown pieces of fat or crackling left after fat pork has been melted down for lard or dripping. Pork butchers in the Midlands, on the Welsh border, and elsewhere sometimes sell them. They should be rescued from obscurity. When made crisp in the oven and rolled in salt they go well with aperitifs.

Fry a small, peeled, diced onion gently in 25 g (1 oz) lard until it begins to turn golden. Then add 225 g (8 oz) sliced mushrooms and 1 teaspoon of chopped fresh parsley. Let this cook, simmering gently with a lid on the pan, until the mushrooms are soft and their black juices are running out. Add 225 g (8 oz) each of roughly chopped lean pork and diced scruggins or crackling. Then mince all the ingredients with about ½ teaspoon salt and a pinch of mixed herbs and mix well. Pack it into a greased terrine and cover the mixture closely with foil.

Stand the terrine on a rack, or an upturned saucer, in a pan with boiling water to come halfway up the sides of the dish. Bring this once more to the boil and cook, bubbling gently with a lid on the pan, for 45 minutes.

Remove the terrine from the pan and chill. The contents are usually served sliced, with rye or wholemeal bread.

Terrine of Quails' Eggs in Aspic

The small mottled cream and brown quails' eggs have a delicate flavour of their own, less strong than that of gulls' eggs. They blend well with some pâtés. To be served with hot French bread and butter.

Line a terrine with a mild, fine-textured liver pâté (page 30). Pour 300 ml (½ pint) tin of consommé into a pan, stir in 2 level teaspoons of powdered gelatine and heat it gently, stirring all the time over a low heat until the gelatine melts. Remove the pan from the heat and let the mixture cool.

Cook 6 quails' eggs in boiling water for 4 minutes, then plunge them into cold water. Shell them and put them in a bowl of cold water.

Stone some plump black olives neatly, and place them on the pâté with the quails' eggs. When the jellied consommé is half set and cold, spoon it over them. Chill in the refrigerator for about 2 hours until set. Remove about 30 minutes before serving.

Hungarian Spiced Hare

A superb dish for a February night from the Bákony Forest. It is turned out to serve cold, usually with a classic potato salad, some bárács palinka (apricot brandy) and a good gutsy red wine.

The hare is pickled in a cooked marinade for at least three days, preferably four. To make this peel and slice 1 carrot and 1 parsnip, and boil them in just over 1 litre (2 pints) of water with 3 bay leaves, 8 peppercorns, and 1 tablespoon of salt. When tender add 300 ml (½ pint) of red wine, the juice of 1 lemon, and 1 tablespoon of sugar. Put the hare in a deep dish, not a metal one, and pour the hot marinade over it.

The hare must be well covered. Keep it in a cool place, straining off the liquor every day, boiling it up and then pouring it back over the meat. After 3 or 4 days put the hare and the marinade in a pan with a lid and let it cook gently till tender, basting it frequently and being careful not to let it brown. When tender, lift it out of the pan; the meat should be dropping off the bones. Cut two long fillets from either side of the back along the whole length and set them aside.

Mince the rest of the hare with 100 g (4 oz) of lean bacon, stir in 1 tablespoon of flour, add salt, pepper, a dash of vinegar and 175 g (6 oz) of finely chopped smoked fat bacon in chunks. Add 3 beaten eggs, 25 g (1 oz) of chopped capers, the grated rind of 1 lemon, and mix well. Put half this forcemeat in an oblong terrine, arrange the fillets of hare on top, and cover with the remaining forcemeat. Cover the terrine with foil, tie down firmly, stand it in a water bath, and bake it in a moderate oven, 180°C (350°F)/Gas 4, for one hour. Let it cool and then chill.

The terrine can be used next day and is often turned out to serve. For this dip the bottom of the terrine in hot water, then turn the contents onto a long cold dish. It is decorated in Hungary with chopped aspic, hard-boiled eggs and rosehip purée or cranberry sauce.

POTTING AND COLLARING

ENGLISH POTTED MEATS were sometimes made as fillings for raised pies but were more usually set in white pottery basins and topped with clarified butter. Grouse, partridge, pigeons, pheasant and even larks and moorhens were potted, often after being marinated in port or brown sherry. In Edwardian England potted meats and fish pastes often appeared for afternoon tea to be spread on hot buttered toast, or served with crumpets. These things also make a good first course for a dinner party, with the hot buttered toast, or with brown bread and butter. They should not, however, be served as part of a mixed *hors d'oeuvre*. English potted meats have a delicate flavour which is different from that of French pâtés, and the various foreign tastes and mixtures of the hors d'oeuvre may well overpower them.

In the nineteenth century potted meats were mostly prepared by cooks at the great country houses, from some of the riper contents of the game larder after there had been several shoots. But family butchers prepared potted meats too, in huge basins often with the words 'potted meat' or 'potted game' printed on them in large black letters. The contents were sold off piecemeal from the back of the shop.

Collaring is an old almost forgotten way of dressing long pieces of meat or fish. It was fashionable in the eighteenth century but now some cookery books describe it as 'a galantine' by mistake. Rather surprisingly, even the Concise Oxford Dictionary notes that a *collar* is (among other things) 'a piece of meat brawn or fish tied in a roll'.

Collared beef is a long slim piece of inexpensive beef flank, pickled in salt, sugar and saltpetre. It is then washed and trimmed, spread with herbs and spices, rolled up, tied first with tape and then in a cloth and boiled. When cooked

67

it is cooled under weights, then glazed with aspic and eaten cold.

The famous Mrs Rundell gives a recipe for collared eels in her *New System of Domestic Cookery* published in 1807. It was a best-seller during most of the nineteenth century. According to Mrs Rundell the eel should be boned but not skinned, spiced and then rolled up and tied with tape and subsequently boiled in salted water 'till enough'. Mackerel, she wrote, could be collared too. There was collared breast of lamb or mutton, which people ate in those days with pickles. It was stuffed with anchovies and then rolled and boiled as before. In eighteenth-century Ireland a popular dish was collared salmon, boned and stuffed with oysters, cream and beaten egg, then rolled up and done in a pot with crumbs and melted butter. It was served hot with parsley sauce.

Potted Ham with Chicken*

This old recipe is equally good when made with cold turkey and ham, or with boiled bacon, instead of the chicken. Quite apart from being delicious it solves the problem of what to do with a piece of gammon or bacon when there is too little left of it to carve. Send in plenty of hot toast.

An electric blender could, if liked, be substituted for the pestle and mortar in the original recipe, which is taken from *The Experienced English Housekeeper* by Mrs Raffald, published in 1789. Twice as much puréed chicken, say 675 g (1½ lb), is required as of lean ham 225 g (8 oz) and fat 100 g (4 oz).

'Take as much lean of a boiled ham as you please, and half the quantity of fat, cut it as thin as possible. Beat it very fine in a mortar with a little oiled butter, mace, pepper and salt. Put part of it into a china pot. Then beat the white part of a (cooked) fowl with a very little seasoning. It is to qualify the ham. Put a layer of fowl, then one of ham, then fowl on top, press hard down and when it is cold pour clarified butter on it. When you send it to table cut out a thin slice in the form of half a diamond and lay it round the edge of your pot.'

Potted Chicken, Partridge or Pheasant

From Eliza Acton's *Modern Cookery for Private Families*, 1845, this recipe is a good way of using cold roast chicken or pheasant.

'Roast the birds as for table, but let them be thoroughly done, for if the gravy be left in, the meat will not keep half so well. Raise the flesh of the breast, wings, and merrythought (wishbone), quite clear from the bones, take off the skin, mince, and then pound it very smoothly with about one third of its weight of fresh butter (unsalted butter), or something less, if the meat should appear of a proper consistence without the full quantity; season it with salt, (powdered) mace, and cayenne (pepper) only, and add these in small portions until the meat is rather highly flavoured with both the last . . . When perfectly pounded, press it into small potting-pans, and pour clarified butter over the top. This should never be poured *hot* on the meat: it should be less than milk warm when added to it . . .'

Potted Hare

In this recipe, also from *Modern Cookery*, Eliza Acton sensibly suggested putting the remains of the hare to good use in a soup.

'When the old fashioned mode of potting is preferred, (the hare) must be cleansed as for roasting, wiped dry, cut into joints, which, after being seasoned with salt, cayenne (or pepper) and pounded cloves and mace or nutmeg well mingled, should be closely packed in a jar or deep pan, and slowly baked until very tender, with the addition of from half to a whole pound of fresh (unsalted) butter laid equally over it, in small bits, the jar must be well covered with at least two separate folds of thick brown paper tied closely over it. It should then be left to become perfectly cold; and the butter should be taken off and scraped free from moisture, that it may be added to the hare in pounding it. All the skin and sinew must be carefully removed, and the flesh minced before it is put into the mortar. Additional seasoning must be added if necessary; but the cook must remember that all should be well blended, and no particular spice should be allowed to predominate in the flavour of the preparation.

'The bones, gravy, head and ribs will make a small tureen of excellent soup. Thick slices of lean ham are sometimes baked with the hare, and pounded with it.'

Moulded Potted Meat or Fish

A third idea from Eliza Acton's *Modern Cookery*.

'Press very closely and smoothly into a pan or mould the potted meat . . . pour a thin layer of clarified butter on the top, and let it become quite cold. When wanted for table, wind round it for a moment a cloth which has been dipped into hot water, loosen the meat gently from it with a thin knife, turn it on to a dish, and glaze it lightly; lay a border of small salad round it, with or without a decoration of hard eggs, or surround it instead with clear savoury jelly cut in dice. The meat, for variety, may be equally sliced, and laid regularly round a pile of small salad. A very elegant second course dish may be made with potted lobsters in this way, the centre being ornamented with a small shape of lobster butter.'

Potted Partridge in Jelly

For the tougher casserole birds, whether grouse, pigeon or partridge; when cold the stock sets in a jelly and the butter rising to the top forms a seal as in potted shrimps.

Put salt, pepper and a spoonful of butter inside each of 2 birds. Pack them in a stone jar, or terrine, or pie dish of suitable size. Add the rest of the butter, to make 100 g (4 oz) altogether for a brace of birds. Pour in enough strong clear jellying stock to cover them completely. This may be home-made or, in an emergency, a tinned consommé. Add a glass of cooking sherry or ruby port. Cover the jar or dish with foil and a lid. Cook in a moderate oven, 180°C (350°F)/Gas 4, for about 2 hours or until the birds are tender. Chill.

The birds should not be uncovered until they are to be

eaten. This is an excellent first course which may be served with hot toast and dry sherry.

Potted Tongues*

These are delicious chilled, in small white pots, to eat with hot buttered toast for tea, or as a first course at dinner. Serve the butter separately, the hot toast wrapped cosily in a napkin.

Put 450 g (1 lb) of lambs' tongues in a pan with salt, pepper, a bay leaf, some mixed herbs and a sliced onion, and add water to cover. Bring this to the boil and let them simmer for about an hour until they are tender.

Trim any gristly bits and hard skin from the tongues, then put the rest through the mincer. Add salt, freshly ground nutmeg and some freshly made English mustard—the powered kind that one mixes with water. Exact quantities depend on individual taste. Then add enough softened butter to make it into a spreadable paste. Pack it all into a terrine, or into little pots. Stand these in a tin with water to come halfway up the sides of the dish and cook in a slow oven, 150°C (300°F)/Gas 2 for a little over ½ hour. Let the potted meat become quite cold, then pour a thin layer of clarified or melted butter over the top.

The same recipe may be used for boiled bacon but with rather less salt, or for the remains of home-cooked ox tongue.

Lambs' Tongues Marbl'd

The recipe dates from 1783, but these little potted tongues were often eaten chilled for tea in Edwardian England, with thin bread and butter. Boil 900 g (2 lb) of lambs' tongues with a pig's foot and 450 g (1 lb) of pickled pork belly, some salt, pepper, and nutmeg until tender. Skin the tongues, bone and chop the pig's foot, and chop the pork belly. As it is pickled the pork belly will be pink, and this gives a marbled effect when mixed with the other meat. Add the jellying stock from the pan, pour the mixture into a basin to set, and chill. Turn it out by dipping the bottom of the basin in warm water.

71

Potted Trout

Clean and then gently fry in butter as many fish as you like. Remove the skins while they are still warm and lift the flesh gently off the bones in sections. Lay these neatly in a buttered pie dish deep enough to hold the trout, sprinkling each layer with a little salt and pepper. Pour melted butter over them to seal, and eat them cold, with toast. Mackerel, too, are excellent when prepared like this.

Potted Char

The char, found in Lake Windermere and some Scandinavian and Austrian lakes, is virtually the same fish as the rare and exquisite *ombre chevalier* found in Lake Annecy and Lake Leman. *Larousse Gastronomique* mentions potted char as 'a fish conserve formerly held in great esteem in England, where it is eaten for breakfast.' The recipe is much the same as that for Potted Trout.

Venison Paste

To be used as a sandwich filling or on hot buttered toast.

This is made in Scotland from about 450 g (1 lb) of odd venison trimmings after making pies and so on, or from the scrag end of venison. Rather more of the latter should be allowed as it is a cut with a lot of bones. Put the boned chopped meat in an ovenproof dish with 6 peppercorns, a blade of mace, a clove, some salt and a *bouquet garni* or pot posy. Add 150 ml (¼ pint) of stock. Cover the dish with foil and cook in a moderate oven, 180°C (350°F)/Gas 4, until very tender. Remove the pot posy or *bouquet garni* and blend the rest of the ingredients to a purée together with 25 g (1 oz) melted butter and a large glass of port. Chill.

Potted Cheshire Cheese*

This is taken from *The Compleat Housewife* by E. Smith, published in 1727. It seems that the glass of sherry was about the size of a small tumbler.

'Take ¾ lb of old Cheshire cheese, shave it all very thin.

Then put it in a mortar and add to it a good pinch of mace, 4 oz of fresh butter, and half a glass of sherry. Mix and beat these together until they are all perfectly incorporated. Then put it in a pot what thickness you please, and cut it in slices for cream cheese, and serve it with the dessert.'

Collared Beef

Put a 2.7 kg (6 lb) piece of beef flank in a large basin, rub it with 175 g (6 oz) of common salt, 25 g (1 oz) of saltpetre, and 50 g (2 oz) of soft brown sugar 'pieces'. Leave this for 7 days in a cool larder. Turn the meat every day, rubbing it with the salt, saltpetre and sugar.

After a week, drain and trim the meat of any gristle, wash it well to get rid of surplus salt, and sprinkle it with a level teaspoon of powdered allspice, a dessertspoon of dried rubbed sage and some freshly ground black pepper. Roll it up, and tie it with tape if available, string if not. Fasten it in a boiling cloth and tie this up tightly.

Put the bones from the meat in a large pan with 2 roughly chopped onions, a sliced carrot, a little celery if available and a large pinch of fresh mixed herbs. Add the meat in its cloth, with enough hot water to cover. Bring it to the boil and let it simmer for 5 hours—in, for instance, the oven of a solid fuel cooker. Take the meat out of the boiling cloth and press it under a weight until cold and set.

The broth in which it cooks should make excellent soup.

Collared Breast of Lamb*

Bone a breast of lamb, cutting off some of the fat. Beat the piece of meat out as flat as possible. Sprinkle it thickly with chopped parsley, sage and sweet basil mixed with ground cloves, freshly grated nutmeg, and salt and pepper. Roll it up, tie it with a piece of tape or string and then fasten it in a cloth. It is important to roll and tie it tightly. Put it in a deep casserole or pan, add the bones and enough water to cover. Let it simmer for about 2 hours, then remove from the pan and press it under a weight until cold. Take off the cloth and, if liked, glaze with the stock, which should set in a jelly (see aspic chapter).

Collared Breast of Veal

This is dressed and cooked in the same way as the breast of lamb, but is simmered in milk and water, and pressed till cold. The meat can then be sliced in neat rounds which look not unlike a Swiss roll.

GALANTINES

A GALANTINE LOOKS MOST IMPRESSIVE on a cold buffet, but is in fact easy to prepare if a little time is taken to do so. Since a small duck or chicken when boned and stuffed will be enough for about ten people, it is also relatively inexpensive. Some poulterers or butchers will bone the bird if warned beforehand, but it is easy to bone at home with a sharp knife, penknife or razor blade.

The word galantine is wrongly used in some cookery books for what is really a meat loaf, and sometimes for a sort of brawn. It is really an elegant cold dish made from boned poultry or game birds (or sometimes meat) stuffed with a fine forcemeat and pressed into a symmetrical shape, cooked, and eaten cold. Some of the old galantines popular in the early nineteenth century in both England and France were made from poultry and game birds of different sizes, boned and laid one inside the other. They might graduate in size from a lark to a goose and were sometimes cooked in enormous terrines with forcemeat filling up any gaps round the edges.

A *ballotine*, on the other hand, is really a sort of galantine to serve hot (though it is often served cold too). It is supposed to be a piece of lean boned stuffed meat rolled up like a bundle. A shoulder of lamb is the joint most often used, though in fact nowadays there are ballotines of poultry and even fish.

Blanc de poulet farci also belongs to the galantine family, being chicken breast and white meat flavoured with cognac, spices and herbs stuffed with forcemeat shaped in the form of a chicken and often garnished with aspic and bay leaves. A *cochonette* is a galantine of boned stuffed suckling pig, served cold in aspic and sometimes garnished with pimiento.

A *zampone* is a delicacy from Modena which is mostly eaten in Italy at Christmas. It is a boned and stuffed, very subtly flavoured pig's foot, which is boiled and then eaten hot or cold in thin slices.

Gerauchertes Gaensebrust, or smoked goose breast, is popular in Germany and Denmark for the cold table, and keeps for 6-8 weeks in the refrigerator.

In Namur in Belgium the *charcutiers* bone a whole goose completely, fill it with a rich forcemeat and cook it in a yeast pastry.

Galantine of Chicken

A 1.2 kg (2½ lb) bird will be enough for nine or ten people. There is no waste, and you just slice it across like pâté or a sausage to reveal a marble mosaic of mushroom and green nuts framed delicately in poultry. Though it does take a little time to prepare, the whole thing is very simple.

If you are boning the bird at home tell the butcher not to truss the chicken, because the skewers will make holes in the skin. Lay the bird breast down on the kitchen table. Using a sharp penknife, scalpel or butcher's knife cut the skin down the middle of the back to the level of the thighs. Ease and cut the meat off the bones as far as the wings and leg joints. Do it almost as if you were removing a pair of long tight kid gloves. Keep the skin whole, but do not bother too much about taking all the meat off the bones. You can cut it off afterwards and put it in the stuffing.

Now cut off the wings at the second joint so that only the last section is left on the bird. Then break off the wing and leg bones from the carcase and ease the meat off them. Leave the drumsticks in the legs. Finally ease the meat off the front of the chicken and lift out the carcase. You will now have a complete bag of chicken rather like a zip-fastening track suit with a pair of drumsticks in it.

Lay it flat on the table, sprinkle the inside with salt, pepper, nutmeg and lemon juice and tuck in the flaps where the wing bones were.

Almost any good, rich, well-flavoured meaty stuffing will do, but it looks more professional if there is a mixture of light and dark, chopped and minced meat.

Mince 225 g (8 oz) of fat unsmoked bacon with 225 g (8 oz) of lean pork, add 150 ml (¼ pint) of red wine, an egg and a

78

little chopped garlic. Mince 225 g (8 oz) of chicken livers and mix them with three tablespoons of the pork and bacon mixture. Lay the two kinds of stuffing in the chicken in strips. Add the chopped meat from the chicken bones, 100 g (4 oz) of salami cut into matchstick strips, two Frankfurter sausages, 50 g (2 oz) of sliced mushrooms and, if you like, a few green pistachio nuts.

Fold the chicken over the stuffing and stitch over the back and the parson's nose with strong thread. Do not try to get it back into its original shape, just lay it in the roasting tin and form it into a kind of sausage-shaped chicken with legs. Lay strips of fat bacon on top, and cover with foil. Roast it for 2½-3 hours in a very moderate oven, 170°C (325°F)/Gas 3. Take off the foil and bacon fat and increase the heat at the end to brown the breast. Remove the bits of sewing thread before serving the galantine cold, nicely garnished and on a suitable dish.

Galantine de Poularde Perigordine

This is a classic galantine from southwest France. The boned stuffed capon is not roasted but poached in a rich jellying stock, which is subsequently used to make aspic with which to glaze and garnish the bird when cold, in the orthodox manner.

Bone a young 2.2 kg (5 lb) capon. Spread it neatly on a board or kitchen table skin side down. Sprinkle it with a little salt and pepper. Chop 675 g (1½ lb) tenderloin of pork and 225 g (8 oz) of cooked ham in 1 cm (½ in) dice. Also chop the liver of the bird, 150 g (5 oz) fat unsmoked bacon and 3 or 4 truffles (if possible) in rather smaller dice. Add the scraps of meat from the carcase, dicing these too. Put all the dice in a basin with 1½ teaspoons salt, a good pinch of *les 4 épices* (page 129), 1 tablespoon of armagnac, and 3 tablespoons of dry white wine and mix it all well.

Spread 450 g (1 lb) of sausagemeat (good pure pork sausagemeat) over the capon. Lay the other coarser mixture evenly on it. Now roll up the capon neatly in the shape of a large sausage. Wrap it in a cloth, tying it firmly at each end and here and there along the length of the roll, but not too tightly as it expands in cooking.

In the bottom of a large pan put 1 peeled sliced carrot and

2 peeled chopped onions, the carcase of the bird broken in pieces, the giblets and 100 g (4 oz) unsalted pork rind or pork belly. Lay the galantine on this. Place 1 split, unsalted pig's foot on either side. Cover the pan and leave the contents over a very, very low heat for 10 minutes. Add 3 litres (3 quarts) water, 150 ml (¼ pint) white wine, a *bouquet garni* tied with cotton, 2 cloves, 1 garlic clove, and 1 teaspoon salt. Simmer, covered, for 2½ hours, then remove the galantine and let it cool.

Let the stock simmer gently for 2 more hours to reduce before straining it through a fine sieve. It will form a jelly when cold. Remove all the fat from it and clear the jellied stock with egg whites (see the chapter on aspic).

When the galantine of capon is cool remove the cloth and place the galantine on a meat dish, breast side down, with a board on top and 2 1 kg (2 lb) weights spaced out on the board. Chill overnight under the weights.

The next day arrange the galantine on a layer of jellied stock or aspic on a suitable oval platter. Spoon more of the aspic over the surface and chill, until it forms a jellied glaze.

Boar's Head*

A Christmas tradition much older than turkey is boar's head, the great Christmas dish of medieval England. In Chaucer's day it used to be carried in by the Lord of the Feast, preceded by his henchmen blowing a fanfare of trumpets and singing an appropriate carol. It was popular, too, in Queen Victoria's day when they used to bring it in to dinner to a military accompaniment of fife and drums.

A pig's head (which is what is used for this stupendous dish) is very cheap. Ask the butcher to pickle it in brine and if possible leave a larger flap of skin at the back than usual—this makes it easier to stuff. Get him to clean it and cut the head in two halves except for a skin joining it at the top, and to take out the big bones at the back of the head. If you only want it to look pretty almost any forcemeat will do so long as it keeps the head well packed to preserve its shape.

A really delicious stuffing is made by mixing 450 g (1 lb) sausagemeat with some diced bacon, a little chopped garlic, a glass of sherry and a raw egg. Fry and mince 225 g (8 oz) of pig's liver and then mix it with 3 tablespoons of the sausagemeat stuffing. Lay the two kinds of stuffing inside the head in strips, add 100 g (4 oz) of mushrooms and a hard-boiled egg. This makes a delicious galantine when carved.

Stitch the pig's head up firmly with button thread, put a lemon in its mouth and tie it up well in an old pillow case. Put it in a pan with cold water to cover and bring it to the boil, skimming off the froth. Add a sliced onion, 2 carrots, 12 peppercorns, 3 cloves, some mixed herbs and, if liked, a bottle of beer to the cooking water.

Simmer till tender, about 6-7 hours, very gently. Let it get cold in the stock (which could then be used for soup), then take off the pillow case. Put the head on a meat dish and glaze it with aspic. In this instance it is best to use a bottle of the commercial kind of aspic powder made up double strength—that is, with only half the normal amount of liquid. When it is cool and thick enough to stick like varnish to a metal spoon, pour it carefully over the pig's head from a small jug. This should be done several times at intervals. There should be about 4 coats. Of course a good home-made aspic may be used but it must set in a very, very stiff jelly and it should be a good dark colour.

Garnish the head with tufts of parsley in the ears, prunes put in for eyes, tusks made from celery and a fresh lemon in the mouth if necessary. A suitably savage expression is achieved by piping furious eyebrows on the beast in savoury butter.

Half a sandwich loaf covered in foil makes a good wedge or cushion with which to steady large pieces of this sort, and a skewer may be thrust up through it to impale the boar's head.

The boar's head looks very Elizabethan if a deep pie frill is put on as a collar behind the ears, like a fat man wearing a ruff. The centre part behind the frill could be covered with foil. A second pie frill may be rolled tightly and pinned and put on the head like a coronet. Long ornamental skewers— what chefs call *hatelets*—if available add greatly to its appearance.

This does not freeze well, but keeps for about fourteen days in the refrigerator.

Cold Turkey with Two Pâtés

The good Baron Brisse gives a rather sketchy recipe in his *Cuisine à l'Usage des Ménages Bourgeois* for a whole boned turkey stuffed with finely pounded and highly seasoned forcemeat of pork and veal, laced with long strips of turkey, pieces of pink pickled pork, whole cornichons, pistachio nuts and truffles 'if one is fortunate enough to have any'. Cold turkey with two pâtés is much simpler to prepare and makes a very good party piece.

Stuff the main turkey cavity with coarse-cut liver pâté with hazelhuts, or *pâté de foie aux pruneaux* (the recipe on page 17 is for about 900 g (2 lb) of pâté). Stuff the crop with fine textured chicken liver pâté such as the Austrian *wiener huehnerleberpastete* (page 30) using the turkey liver and some chicken livers to make it.

Sew up or skewer the turkey. Butter the bird all over thickly, and sprinkle it with salt and pepper. Roast it for 20 minutes per 450 g (1 lb) and 20 minutes over in a moderate oven, 180°C (350°F)/Gas 4, with a piece of foil laid loosely over the breast. Pour a glass of water under the bird and baste occasionally. Add another if it has mostly evaporated. In calculating the weight of the turkey for roasting do not forget to include the weight of the stuffing and, if it was a frozen bird, be sure it has thawed completely right inside before cooking it. This takes 48 hours, and sometimes longer at room temperature.

To see if the turkey is cooked thrust a fork deep into the thigh; if the gravy runs out clear the bird is cooked. Serve it cold, slicing some of the pâté from the crop and some of that from inside, and serving these with the meat. This is excellent for a party. Cumberland sauce (page 124) may be served with it, and one can make little frills of foil to go round the bird's ankles.

Galantine de Faisan ou Pintadeau

The galantine can be made with pheasant or guinea fowl if one adjusts the amount of forcemeat to the size of the bird. 900 g (2 lb) of forcemeat is generally considered about enough for the average chicken, but a pheasant will take less. The bird should not be too well hung as it will then be almost impossible to bone it and leave the skin intact.

Having boned the bird, put the meatless carcase in a large pan with any giblets, chicken bones, butchers' bones or a ham bone according to what is available. Add 2 unsalted split pigs' feet, 1 chopped onion, 1 sliced carrot, 12 crushed juniper berries, 2 cloves, 2 tablespoons of Plymouth gin, ½ bottle of dry white wine and a little stock from chicken bouillon cubes to cover. Bring it to the boil and simmer gently for 2 hours.

Meanwhile marinate 175 g (6 oz) diced cooked ham and the pheasant liver in a little sherry overnight. The next day, make a forcemeat from equal parts of lean and fat meat. Mince 225 g (8 oz) fat pork with any pheasant trimmings off the carcase, 75 g (3 oz) of lean pork, 1 level teaspoon allspice or *les 4 épices* (page 129), 6 crushed juniper berries, a little salt and some freshly ground black pepper. Stir in the diced meats and liquor from the marinade with 2 small beaten eggs, to make a marbled effect.

Lay the boned pheasant skin down on the kitchen table. Sprinkle it with salt, pepper and a little Plymouth gin, and wrap it round the prepared forcemeat. Stitch it up the back and wrap it in kitchen foil and a cloth. Tie on the cloth firmly but leave enough space for the galantine to expand in cooking. Poach it in the prepared stock, gently simmering, for about 1¾ hours. Cool under weights as usual.

When cold coat it with aspic made from the cleared stock and garnish it in the appropriate manner.

Galantine of Pigeons*

Take 2 plucked cleaned pigeons. It does not matter if they are only casserole birds so long as they have been cleaned neatly, with no gaping holes and almost all the skin intact.

Make a cut down the backs of the birds, and with a sharp knife and your fingers loosen the flesh from each side of the carcase. Be careful not to make a hole in the skin. It does not matter if some of the meat is left on the bones; it can be cut off later and added to the stuffing. Lay the birds breast down and wide open and lift out the carcases in one piece. Poultry scissors are helpful. The thigh bones should really be eased out but if you have not had much practice and find this difficult leave them in. The drumsticks and wing bones are left in anyway.

Lay the skin and flesh as flat as possible. Sprinkle it with salt, pepper and old brown cooking sherry, and leave the pigeons to marinate while boiling down the carcases to make stock. To do this, break up the carcases, put them in a pan with 1 sliced onion, salt, pepper, herbs and enough water to cover. Either simmer for 1½ hours or cook them for 30 minutes in the pressure cooker.

For the stuffing mix 450 g (1 lb) of good sausagemeat with a clove of peeled chopped garlic, 12 crushed juniper berries, the pigeons' livers chopped, any pigeon meat (also chopped), and 100 g (4 oz) chopped mushrooms. Stuff the birds, sew them up, and wrap each one in vine leaves and a bacon rasher. Tie them with string. It is best if the vine leaves are fresh or from the freezer. If tinned, or taken from some sort of pickle, they must be well washed and rinsed before use. Strain the carcase stock, bring it to the boil, put in the birds, and simmer for 30 minutes. Plunge them in ice cold water, and when cold remove the string, bacon and vine leaves. Garnish them with aspic, stoned grapes and fresh vine leaves. Aioli (page 123) is delicious with them.

MOUSSES

MOUSSES ARE NOW very popular at parties, being easy to eat with a fork. Once very elaborate, these days they are served casually and simply in white pottery soufflé dishes, either plain or topped with aspic. Some are made in little pots and turned out to serve, garnished perhaps with sliced lemon and watercress, or button mushrooms and radishes.

On a hot day a light and fluffy cold mousse makes a perfect meal, or a fresh and simple first course for a dinner party. They are relatively inexpensive, too, since 450 g (1 lb) of cold chicken or turkey will make an elegant mousse for about twelve people.

Cheddar Mousse*

A light delicate summery start to a meal served in little pottery ramekin dishes, to be eaten with a spoon. Thin brown bread and butter make a nice, but by no means necessary accompaniment.

Beat 2 egg yolks until they are pale and trickle off the whisk in ribbons. Add 50 g (2 oz) grated cheese, a pinch of salt, 1 heaped teaspoon of English mustard powder, and a little freshly grated nutmeg. Beat, then add 300 ml (½ pint) of stiffly whipped double cream. Finally fold in the whites of the 2 eggs, so stiffly whipped that the basin may be turned upside down without them falling out. Spoon into 4 ramekin dishes, and chill.

Chicken Mousse*

This is a convenient way of using the remains of a cold chicken or turkey. Quantities may be doubled for a large number of people and set in two soufflé dishes or a huge 2.5 litre (5 pint) one. It freezes well without the aspic topping;

87

this should only be added after the mousse has come out of the freezer and has thawed.

Make a purée of 225 g (8 oz) of cooked chicken or turkey in the liquidiser, together with 2 tablespoons of milk or of broth from the giblets and carcase. Make a thick white sauce by melting 1 tablespoon of butter, stirring in 1 tablespoon of flour, then gradually adding 300 ml (½ pint) of poultry broth (or of milk). Heat, stirring, until the sauce is smooth and thick. Add 15 g (½ oz) gelatine powder dissolved in a tablespoon of warm water, stirring until very well mixed. When the mixture has cooled slightly stir in 2 egg yolks, the chicken purée and, later, 3 tablespoons of thick homemade mayonnaise. Taste for seasoning, adding salt, pepper and a little freshly grated nutmeg and powdered tarragon if liked. Whip the whites of the 2 eggs so stiffly that the basin may be turned upside down without them falling out. Stir the chicken mixture and fold these in gently. Put it all in a 1.25 litre (2½ pint) soufflé dish to set. Garnish the top with bay leaves.

Make up 600 ml (1 pint) of aspic (preferably from the carcase stock). Let it cool and thicken until it is almost a jelly, then pour it very gently over the chicken mousse. Chill till set. If the aspic is added when still runny small bits of chicken tend to detach themselves and float in it to make the jelly cloudy.

Crab Mousse

This is at its best when made with the meat of a freshly cooked crab and looks delicious when chilled in a ring mould and turned out to serve. Garnish the sides of the dish with hunks of lemon and the legs and claws of the crab, and fill the centre of the mould with a bunch of watercress. Cold avocado sauce, which is a delicate green, is most acceptable with it.

Flake 225 g (8 oz) of crab meat or more if available, both brown and white. Add 2 egg yolks, 1 tablespoon of grated cheese, 1 tablespoon of cooking sherry, the juice and grated rind of 1 lemon and ½ teaspoon of curry powder. Mix well and blend to a purée in the liquidiser. Add 1 tablespoon of mayonnaise, 300 ml (½ pint) cool aspic jelly and a teaspoon of paprika powder to make it pink. When cold and setting fold in 2 very stiffly whipped egg whites. Chill.

For the avocado sauce peel and stone 3 avocados, and blend the flesh with the juice of 1 lemon, 1 crushed garlic clove and 300 ml (½ pint) of soured cream in the liquidiser until smooth. Season with salt and pepper. Cover the dish well and chill. This sauce is enough for ten people. It can be kept in the refrigerator overnight without changing colour if you cover the dish closely with plastic cling wrap.

Cucumber and Cream Cheese Mousse*

For six people peel half a cucumber and dice it very finely. Mix it with 15 g (½ oz) of caster sugar and 3 tablespoons of white wine vinegar. Leave it to absorb the flavours. Beat up 175 g (6 oz) of cream cheese. Add salt and white pepper to taste.

Melt a 15 g (½ oz) packet of gelatine in 3 tablespoons of hot water. Let it cool slightly, then fold it into the cheese together with the well drained diced cucumber. Whip 150 ml (¼ pint) of double cream absolutely stiff and when the cream cheese and cucumber is beginning to set fold it in. Finally, fold in the whites of 3 eggs which have been whisked so stiffly that the basin may be turned upside down without them falling out. Put it into a mould and leave it in the fridge to set. This looks very pretty decorated on top with sprigs of cress and twists of cucumber. It is served with hot toast.

Egg Mousse*

Press the yolks of six hard-boiled eggs through a sieve, chop the egg whites and mix both together. Whip 150 ml (¼ pint) of double cream. Mix 300 ml (½ pint) of hot water with 15 g (½ oz) of powdered gelatine and a chicken stock cube. Heat gently in a pan until all is melted and the liquid is clear. Chill until it is half setting and has thickened a little, then pour it all at once on to the eggs with the whipped cream and stir it at once to make an even mixture. Add salt, pepper, and Worcestershire sauce to your taste. Pour the mousse into a serving dish, smooth over the top to make it even, cover it with foil and chill.

When it is set, garnish the top with a little mound of 'caviar'—the small black granules of Danish lumpenfish roe.

La Mousse de Foie de Volaille

This is a most delicate feather-light mousse, the recipe for which was given to me by M. Francois Bise, proprietor of the famous Auberge du Père Bise at Talloires by Lake Annecy in France.

Trim 225 g (8 oz) of chicken livers, dice 100 g (4 oz) of fat bacon and marinate both overnight in 150 ml (¼ pint) of port with salt, freshly ground black pepper and a small bunch of thyme, parsley and bay leaf. Next morning, remove the bunch of herbs and just stiffen the poultry livers and bacon in a little butter. Then put them through the mincer, fine plates. Line a terrine with thin unsmoked bacon rashers and fill it with the chicken liver mixture. Fold over the ends of the bacon rashers, and cover the top of the terrine with foil and a lid. Stand it in a tin with enough hot water to come halfway up the sides of the terrine and bake it in a moderate oven, 180°C (350°F)/Gas 4 for 45 minutes. It is done when a metal skewer or steel knitting needle thrust in the middle comes out clean.

When it is cold remove the fat above and around the pâté mixture. Take 350 g (12 oz) of *foie gras,* mix both together and press the whole thing through a sieve. Fold in about 2 table-spoons of double cream to bind the whole. Put it in a mould —or, for instance, a white china soufflé dish—and chill it overnight in the refrigerator.

La Mousse de Foie de Volaille can be served with a *gelée au porto.* A dry white wine from the Haute Savoie such as *Aprémont* or *Crépey* would also be pleasant to drink with it.

Smoked Haddock or Cod Mousse*

Cook 225 g (8 oz) of smoked fillet gently in an ample 300 ml

(½ pint) of milk. Peel and roughly chop 2 hard-boiled eggs. Skin and mash the fish, keeping the milk.

Melt 1 tablespoon butter, stir in 1 tablespoon flour, and gradually add the fish and milk, heating, and stirring till the sauce is smooth and thick. Add a little pepper, a good pinch of nutmeg, a small tin of thick cream or a little carton of soured cream, and the chopped eggs.

Make up 300 ml (½ pint) of aspic jelly, stir in a couple of spoonfuls and tip the fish mixture into a white soufflé dish. Chill in the fridge or freezer. When the mousse has set, pour the rest of the now cold aspic gently over the top, pouring it across the back of a tablespoon as one does the cream for Irish coffee (otherwise it makes a hole in the fish mixture). Chill and serve.

Ham and Chicken Mousse*

Fill a deep dish or large soufflé dish with cold ham mousse to within a third of the top. Chill it until set. When it is firm lay neat slices of cooked chicken over it, cover these well with aspic and chill it again till set.

For the mousse, make a purée of 225 g (8 oz) of lean boiled ham or boiled bacon in the liquidiser together with 150 ml (¼ pint) of white sauce, adding a teaspoonful of tomato purée to introduce a nice pink colour. Melt 15 g (½ oz) of powdered gelatine in 150 ml (¼ pint) of stock, and add this little by little, mixing well. When all this is cold and beginning to set, fold in 150 ml (¼ pint) of stiffly whipped double cream and then 2 egg whites that have been whipped so stiffly that the basin may be turned upside down without them falling out. Pile the mousse into the soufflé dish and when set garnish as above.

Smoked Salmon Mousse

This delicious mousse is made with the offcuts and small pieces which are left after slicing a side of smoked salmon, and are sometimes to be had cheaply from delicatessens or good fishmongers. The mousse is then well worth making.

It's difficult to say exactly what weight of salmon pieces to buy because the amounts of skin and bone will vary. Aim at one large cup of salmon bits, and make these into a purée in the blender with a squeeze of lemon juice and a small teaspoon of paprika pepper (not Cayenne) to give it a nice colour. Lightly add or fold in an equal amount of stiffly whipped cream and then add three tablespoons of liquid aspic jelly. Pour the mixture into a soufflé dish.

If the mousse is for a very grand occasion, sprinkle the top with a layer of Danish caviar-style lumpenfish roe, or with very thinly sliced lemon rings. Put it in the fridge. When set pour the rest of the aspic, now cool, over the top. Do this over the back of a tablespoon as one does with the cream in Irish coffee to prevent the aspic from making a hole in the mixture and sinking to the bottom.

South Carolina Shrimp Mousse

This is from *Charleston Receipts*, collected by the Junior League of Charleston, South Carolina, and published in 1951.

'The very small shrimp,' they say, 'caught in the creeks and inlets abounding in the Carolina Low Country are most delicious. They cannot be purchased from the markets but from the negro hucksters who cry their wares through the old city's streets: "swimpee, raw, raw, swimpee!" These shrimp give local recipes that extra flavour and distinction so much enjoyed . . .'

What the Americans call shrimps we in England usually call prawns—which will have to be substituted in the mousse recipe here.

Put 2 egg yolks, a 300 ml (½ pint) can of consommé, 1 dessertspoon French mustard and 100 g (4 oz) butter in the top of a double boiler with hot but not quite boiling water in the pan below. Heat it gently, stirring until the mixture is thick enough to coat the back of a wooden spoon. It must be stirred all the time and it must not boil as it would then curdle.

Stir in 1 stick of very finely chopped celery, 1 very finely chopped paprika pepper without the seeds and 350 g (12 oz) of shelled chopped shrimps—or prawns. Melt 15 g (½ oz) gelatine in 3 tablespoons of hot water, stir this in, and let it all cool. Whip the whites of the 2 eggs so stiffly that the basin may be turned upside down without them falling out, fold them into the mixture, and pour everything into a wetted mould. Chill. Turn it out, when set, to serve garnished with strips of green paprika pepper and a tomato jelly.

To make the tomato jelly, put 2 standard-sized tins of tomato juice in a pan with 6 peppercorns, a piece of garlic or a small chopped onion, 1 bay leaf, and a little dried basil. Bring it to the boil and simmer for about 15 minutes, until the liquid is reduced to 600 ml (1 pint). Stir in 15 g (½ oz) powdered gelatine and 2 teaspoons of tarragon vinegar. Wipe out a mould with a cloth dipped in a little salad oil. Strain the tomato jelly into the mould, and chill till set. Turn it out to serve chopped.

Smoked Trout Mousse

Denis Hine, the landlord of the Three Cocks Hotel, Breconshire, is a member of the famous cognac distilling family. His wife, Madame Baba Hine, gave me this recipe.

Poach 3 smoked trout in enough white wine to cover (about 300 ml (½ pint) for three trout), add a sprig of parsley, a very little chopped onion, 2 bay leaves, a pinch of garlic, a large pinch of tarragon, a small one of thyme and plenty of salt and pepper. Remove the cooked trout, then heat the wine they were cooked in until it is reduced by two-thirds and becomes very highly flavoured. Put this on one side to cool while you take the skin and all the bones out of the smoked trout, which are then put in the liquidiser with the strained cooking liquor. Blend to a purée and whip it up, then add 450 ml (¾ pint) of very stiffly whipped cream, mix and chill.

Cold Woodcock Mousse

Remove the bones and skin from 4 roasted woodcock. Use these to make game stock and hence game aspic. Chop the meat coarsely with a kitchen knife held at both ends. Add half as much *pâté de foie gras*. Taste for seasoning, and then press it all through a fine sieve, working the resulting purée over a bowl of ice, and blending in 25 ml (1 fl oz) of whipped double cream and 2 tablespoons of aspic jelly—preferably made from the very reduced game stock.

Line a mould with aspic, let it partially set, then pour out the still liquid centre. Decorate with sliced truffle. Add the woodcock mousse, filling in any cavities with some of the half liquid aspic. Chill.

Unmould on a solid block of ice, which can easily be made in a domestic freezer—for instance in a well scrubbed roasting tin or suitably shaped mould, shallow biscuit tin, etc. Dip the tin or mould quickly in warm water, then turn it out. The mousse, though very expensive, is delicious and will be enough to serve eight.

ASPIC AND GARNISHES

IT IS IMPORTANT how a dish is presented. Just as oxtail soup would be unpleasant in pewter tankards and champagne disappointing if served in soup cups, so the presentation of a dish makes all the difference to one's enjoyment of it.

Elaborate garnishes are unfashionable and make the food seem contrived and plastic-flavoured. Piped mashed potato and so on is even more unpleasant than a lot of untidy lettuce. Casual elegance is perhaps rather more difficult to achieve in food than in clothes. When, in March 1977, I lunched at the famous Pyramide restaurant in Vienne, many of the dishes had been garnished with small clusters of flowers rather than with parsley or watercress as elsewhere. It looked charming and also very simple, but was of course nothing of the sort. The *pâté de foie gras en brioche,* glazed and with truffles, was flanked by a bunch of polyanthus; the *mousse de truite* in its long copper dish was set on a silver platter garnished with mixed spring flowers. This is something which is difficult to do with conviction, but Madame Point, who has been there for forty years, expects perfection. It made the food look beautiful and was perhaps the equivalent of the expensive little black dress by Pierre Balmain which flatters the wearer and looks deceptively simple.

A little aspic gives a lovely, cool and glamorous appearance to all kinds of potentially unassuming dishes.

Aspic is often poured into pâtés and terrines, for it not only increases their flavour (and corresponds to what in *la grande cuisine* is called a *fumet*) but it also makes the different ingredients cohere as they set, and so the pâté is easier to cut in neat slices.

Aspic is used as a glossy top for some pâtés and mousses, and to coat a galantine or boar's head. It is also added to *pâtés en croûte* and meat pies after they are cooked, through a hole in the top of the pie crust with the aid of a funnel. Chopped aspic is often seen as a garnish for galantines and

97

other cold dishes, hiding any imperfections around the edges.

Most cookery books make very heavy weather of aspic, clarifying it with chopped raw beef, etc., and straining it through muslins (which one never has to hand). In consequence most aspic in Britain is bought ready-made in powder form. This does not taste as good as the real thing.

It is easy to make clear, sparkling, beautifully flavoured aspic in domestic quantities from ordinary household stock, even if it looks ominously thick and cloudy at first. Excellent aspic can be made, for instance, from the carcase and giblets of a roasted chicken, from fish bones and trimmings—sole, turbot and salmon trimmings make a particularly delicious *gelée de poissons*—or from butchers' bones and pigs' feet, with the usual herbs and soup vegetables. It can be made either gently in a large pan, or rapidly in the pressure cooker.

Aspic is easy to clear with the shells and whipped whites of 2 eggs, using the yolks to make mayonnaise or aioli, if liked. It is easy to strain a generous litre (2 pints) of aspic (which is really all that is required domestically) through a wet tea towel laid over a kitchen sieve, or through a Melitta coffee filter and filter paper.

Aspic cannot be frozen at all, however—it goes leathery and tough and often shrinks disastrously as well. Though this can be less noticeable when it has been stirred into the body of a pâté than when it is used as a topping, the well-known wishy-washy and watery texture of pâtés that have been stored in the freezer may be in part due to the degeneration of the aspic. If mousses and so on which are to be served topped with a layer of aspic are to be frozen, then the aspic should only be added after they have come out of the freezer and thawed. Ironically, those commercial pâtés which have been vacuum-packed seem to freeze much better than the home-made ones, perhaps because there is no evaporation.

Aspic

To make aspic from scratch, the first thing you will need is a good stock. This recipe uses a chicken stock.

Rinse a chicken carcase and bones, break them up with your hands and put them in a pan with the giblets, 1 sliced onion, some herbs, 12 peppercorns and 1 teaspoon of salt. Add about 1.5 lites (2½ pints) of water and bring it to the boil. Let it simmer gently with a lid on for about an hour. Strain it into a basin and chill.

When the stock is cold lift off all the fat, wasting some stock if necessary, and remove any fine particles with a spoon or piece of paper, for they make the aspic greasy. Pour the stock through a sieve into a clean rinsed pan. Add 2 15 g (½ oz) packets of powdered gelatine for 1 generous litre (2 pints) of stock and heat, stirring, until it melts completely. Add 2 washed, crushed egg shells and the whites of the two eggs lightly whipped. Bring it all gently to the boil, then let it boil fiercely for a couple of minutes while whisking to make it foamy. It will not look at all clear yet, but have patience. Take it off the heat, put a lid on it and leave it for 10-15 minutes. Now strain the stock through a filter paper such as that used in a Melitta coffee pot. To do this, fit the paper into the pottery strainer top, and stand it on a large jug. Pour in the stock and let it trickle through.

If it is not absolutely clear, strain it again, but do not remove the deposit in the filter as it acts as an extra strainer.

If there is no Melitta filter paper available, 3 or 4 thicknesses of white paper table napkins or paper towels laid in a sieve can sometimes be used instead, the number of thicknesses depending on the quality of the paper. A large clean white handkerchief wrung out in cold water and laid over a sieve on top of a jug makes another substitute.

Cool the aspic in the refrigerator; it will be ready for use when it is half set. It is prepared in exactly the same way with fish stock, or lamb or chicken broth, or whatever. That's all there is to it.

The left-over egg yolks may be used to make mayonnaise.

Aspic powder is sold in packets with full instructions. One simply melts the contents of the packet in warm water (usually one packet per 600 ml (1 pint)) and then lets it simmer over a low heat until the mixture becomes transparent, but without letting it boil. Cool, then chill it until the jelly sets.

For a wine jelly the quantity of water is replaced

proportionately by white wine, port, sherry or Madeira. Opened packets must be used at once. Keep them in a cool dry place.

Quick aspic jelly can also be made by mixing 300 ml (½ pint) of clear meat or chicken stock (made with water and a cube) with a further 300 ml (½ pint) of hot water and 1 teaspoon of meat extract. Add 15 g (½ oz) of powdered gelatine to this and heat, stirring, until it has melted and the stock is perfectly clear.

Aspic jelly can also be made with tinned consommé if 15 g (½ oz) of powdered gelatine is added for every 600 ml (1 pint) of liquid. Add a little port or sherry for flavour and let it set. If the aspic is too stiff, add a little more port or sherry. If it is too thin add a little powdered gelatine and heat, stirring, until it is clear.

Gelatine

One can buy old-fashioned sheet gelatine. This is best torn or cut in pieces with scissors, and must be soaked in cold water before it is melted in the usual way in hot liquid. Ten perfect sheets of gelatine equal 25 g (1 oz); if the sheets are torn, one must of course weigh them.

Nowadays powdered gelatine is mostly used. One 15 g (½ oz) packet is normally enough to set 600 ml (1 pint) of liquid. Reference should be made, though, to the manufacturer's instructions. Different makes may vary in strength.

The best results with gelatine are obtained by melting it first in cold water, just enough to let it swell. Then put the cup or whatever you have used in a saucepan containing a little water. Cook it gently until the mixture becomes syrupy. You can then strain it easily into whatever dish you are making.

When adding gelatine to an already cold mixture, be careful to cool it a little before mixing the two, or you might find the warm gelatine goes lumpy when it comes in contact with the cold mixture. It is also better to add the mixture to the gelatine instead of the other way round. Do this gradually.

Calf's Foot Jelly

Real calf's foot jelly, used so much in *la grande cuisine* (and prescribed in Victorian England for invalids of almost all types), is becoming nearly impossible to make at home. Calves' feet are very difficult to buy, for they go primarily to the catering trade. The dressed cowheel which is sold by butchers and tripe dressers in the north of England will, however, make an excellent jelly, which should be cleared like aspic.

Take 2 calves' feet or 1 dressed cowheel, wash them and cut them in pieces, removing any fat and bone marrow as far as possible. Put them in a pan, cover them with cold water and bring to the boil, then throw this water away.

Now add 2.2 litres (2 quarts) of cold water, 12 peppercorns, and a bay leaf, but no salt until after it is cooked and reduced. To give it a good colour some Irish cooks reduce the quantity of cooking water to 1.7 litres (3 pints) and add 600 ml (1 pint) of strong, strained milkless tea. It does very little for the flavour. Cover the pot and let it sin.mer gently for 5-6 hours; this is especially easy in a solid fuel cooker. The liquid should be reduced to a little less than half. Add a little salt, pour it through a strainer, chill it and then lift off all the fat. Put it in a pan with the thinly peeled rind of 3 lemons and the strained juice of the lemons mixed with enough dry white wine to make this up to 450 ml (¾ pint). Taste for seasoning. Add the crushed shells and whipped whites of 2 eggs, cook and clear it as for aspic jelly (page 98). Turn it into a mould and leave it to set.

If, when cold and de-fatted, the jelly from the cowheel is not sufficiently set, 7 g (¼ oz)—usually half a packet—gelatine may be stirred into the lemon juice and white wine and heated with the stock.

Aspic as a Garnish

Very elegant and even amusing designs can be made by garnishing chilled food with vegetables and so on set in aspic.

Prepare the decorative materials as suggested below, cutting them into the appropriate shapes and chilling them.

When you are ready to use them, spoon two or three layers of aspic jelly over the chilled food which is to be garnished. Hold each piece of garnish with two steel knitting needles or skewers, dip it into the remaining—and almost set—jelly and arrange it on the food. Be sure that small pieces will not detatch themselves and float off when dipped in the jelly. Chill to set the designs, pour over a final coat or two of aspic to cover the decorations with a shimmering transparent layer of aspic, and chill again.

Many foods can be used in this way. A few nice garnishes are:

Black: Truffles or, less extravagantly, thin slices of black olives or pickled walnuts.

White: Strips or dice of hard-boiled egg white.

Yellow: Hard-boiled egg yolks mashed with a little butter.

Red: Small pieces of tinned red pimento.

Green: The green tops of spring onions or leeks softened in hot water, refreshed in cold, then dried and cut in strips.

Chopped aspic also looks very pretty as a garnish and is easy to do. Just let it set in a clean shallow dish, then chop it with a wet knife in strips or chunks and use it as you think fit.

To make jelly cut-outs to put round the edge of a dish, chill a 1 cm (½ in) layer of aspic in a plate or, for instance, a Swiss roll tin. Then cut the aspic in squares, diamonds, or triangles and it is ready for use.

Aspic as a Coating

Let the aspic jelly cool, then chill it (or stir it over cracked ice) until it is almost setting. This is the point at which it will provide the nicest finish when used as a glaze.

Put the galantine, or whatever it may be, on a sieve or on one of those wire cake racks, over a dish. Then spoon the now almost setting aspic jelly over it evenly again and again. Some of the aspic will run down on to the dish below; this can be scooped up and used again. It is a good idea to chill only a little aspic jelly at a time, as the food nearly always needs several coats to achieve a good finish. Leave the jelly to set between coatings.

If the galantine, or cold turkey, or boar's head is to be

decorated with small cut vegetables and truffles, there will have to be one coating to fix the decorations and then, later, a second coat to glaze them.

If you are going to make a pâté which you will unmould to serve, first line the mould with aspic. To do this, rinse a soufflé dish, basin or mould with water, pour it all away, then fill the dish with liquid aspic. Chill it in the refrigerator or freezer. It will set first at the sides. When the sides have set and the middle part is still runny, pour off the excess. The mould can be filled with pâté, or sliced mushrooms, or cooked chicken livers, etc., which should be fixed with some of the remaining aspic. Chill, then turn out to serve.

Liver Pâté in Aspic

Pour 1 litre (1¾ pints) of aspic jelly into a 1.5 litre (2½ pint) soufflé dish and chill. When the sides have set, pour out the still liquid middle part and set aside. Put about 350 g (12 oz) of liver pâté on top of the jelly. Pour the viscous half-setting aspic jelly around the edges of the pâté, and chill. Dip the base of the mould in hot water for a moment and turn it out on to a dish. Serve with hot garlic bread.

Cheese in Aspic

Line a mould with aspic jelly as before. Mix 225 g (8 oz) rich cream cheese (not cottage cheese) with 100 g (4 oz) Danish Blue cheese, 1 tablespoon of sherry, a dash of Tabasco and 1 dessertspoon of Worcestershire sauce. Mash it and blend it well. Put this in the mould lined with aspic jelly when the sides have set. Cover the top and sides with the remaining half-setting aspic jelly. Chill. Unmould it and serve it with Melba toast or garlic toast. It looks well in an oblong mould.

Foies de Volaille en Gelée

Line a 1.5 litre (2½ pint) soufflé dish with aspic jelly as before. Having trimmed 225 g (8 oz) of chicken livers of any stringy or discoloured bits, rinse and pat them dry. Marinate them for an hour in a little salt, freshly ground black pepper, 2 tablespoons of red wine and a peeled chopped garlic clove. Fry them in a little butter rapidly with their liquor till the wine has evaporated and the livers are cooked but pink inside. Turn them on to a clean tea towel, pat them dry, and when cold put them in the lined mould and fill with aspic jelly as before. Chill till set, unmould as before.

Eggs, vegetables and *charcuterie* of your choice can also be arranged in layers with aspic. When the jelly is cold and clear but still runny, pour it into a wetted mould to a thickness of 1 cm (½ in) and chill till set in the refrigerator.

Dip the pieces of pâté, ham, potted meat or fish, egg, or vegetable into the remaining unchilled liquid which has not been in the refrigerator. Arrange them carefully on top of the set layer of aspic. Continue until the mould is full. Put it in the refrigerator to set.

Dip the mould into hot water just before serving. Put a plate on top of it and reverse the mould on to the plate to turn it out. Remove the mould and garnish as desired.

OTHER THINGS

THIS CHAPTER IS, in fact, composed of recipes that I have been unable to fit in elsewhere, but for dishes which are used on many of the same occasions as a pâté. They come from all over Europe—Provence, Italian Umbria, Budapest, Dijon, Blackburn, Montignac and so on—and are mostly much loved and traditional dishes in their places of origin. To me one of the pleasures of a foreign holiday is the visits one pays, perhaps when it is raining or for want of something else to do, to the little old-fashioned food shops in dark side streets, small places with bunches of blackened hams and strange sausages hanging from the ceiling, exotic cheeses on the counter and barrels of olives, anchovies and pickled cucumbers in the back of the shop. This is enjoyable not only for what one buys, and for the strange foods one is often allowed to taste, but for the odd scraps of information and the recipes—perhaps for a local delicacy—that one is given. Even when the *specialité de la maison* turns out to be much the same as that in a shop further down the street, or in another village ten miles off, there are usually subtle family differences. No two *charcutiers* ever seem to prepare exactly the same *pâté, andouilles, boudins* or *salades de boeuf,* any more than the wine from one vineyard is the same as that from the one on the other side of the hill.

Brandade de Morue*

Dried salt cod is cheap, will keep for a long time without a refrigerator, is not difficult to find and has a very unusual taste. It is almost forgotten in this country but is the same as the much loved *morue* of France and the *bacalhão* of Portugal. We used to send it as an outward cargo to Oporto on the ships which would return with casks of port, so that it became popular there. It is used for the great Provençal delicacy *brandade de morue*. White, fluffy and delicious, it makes an excellent first course served hot on plates with a fork. Not everyone cares for the smell while it is cooking.

Soak 450 g (1 lb) of dried salt cod for 24 hours in cold water. Then put it in a pan of boiling water and let it simmer for 20 minutes very gently. Drain it and flake off any skin or bones; there are not many. Put it in the electric blender with 1 large peeled chopped garlic clove and 2 tablespoons of olive oil. Reduce it to a purée.

Meanwhile, as the mixture gradually becomes smooth, pour in a teacup of warm milk little by little and one of warm olive oil, slowly, a spoonful at a time. This should result in a thick white purée, rather like mashed potato. Add some black pepper and a little freshly grated nutmeg, then at the end add a teaspoon of lemon juice. It should be served warm, not hot. If the mixture has gone cold heat the *brandade* gently in the top of a double saucepan over simmering water, or in a pan standing in a larger pan containing simmering water.

Anchoyade

Roughly chop 100 g (4 oz) tinned anchovy fillets (two little tins), put them in the electric liquidiser with their oil, 2 peeled and roughly chopped garlic cloves, and a large teaspoon of tomato paste. Add 1½ tablespoons olive oil, some basil, a little pepper, and a scant dessertspoon of lemon juice or wine vinegar. Blend to a purée, which should be thick like mayonnaise. Toast about ten thick slices from a French loaf on one side and while still warm spread the anchoyade on the plain side.

Eat these at once. Anchoyade is salty and thirstmaking, and goes well with rough red wine from the Roussillon.

Crostini*

The labels on bottles of Orvieto from the vineyards of the Marchese Antinori show a castle standing on a hill surrounded by vines. It was here, at the Castello della Sala, that the Marchese's cook served me these simple but delicious tit-bits, and then gave me the recipe.

Crostini are made by chopping half an onion finely and frying it gently in about 25 g (1 oz) of butter. Add 2 tablespoons of white wine and let it simmer very gently. In another pan cook about 225 g (8 oz) of chicken livers in olive oil with a little chopped fresh sage leaves and salt—just a little of these things, to taste. Then mince the chicken livers and mix them with a tablespoon of capers and 2 chopped anchovy fillets. Stir this into the pan with the browned onion and cook for about 2 minutes before adding about half a teacup of broth (or water and a cube). Let this simmer till it all thickens into a kind of sauce.

Cut some crusty Continental bread in thick slices, moisten these with a little of the broth, and spread the chicken liver mixture over it. You can eat these in your fingers.

Liptoi*

This is a mound of pink and spicy cream cheese popular in the big old-fashioned cafés of Budapest and Vienna for a snack or light informal lunch. They serve it, unmixed, on a white dish with the butter and cheese in the middle and all the other ingredients heaped round them. You mix it yourself with a fork at table so as to get the proportions to your liking and add a little of the beer you are drinking to make it nicely spreadable. It is very good with dark rye bread and a large glass of beer. Put 225 g (8 oz) cream cheese and 225 g (8 oz) of butter on a platter flanked by little separate heaps of chopped parsley, chives, onions, caraway seeds and anchovies. Add a little heap of French mustard and another with at least 2 tablespoons of paprika powder.

A popular mixture is 1 teaspoon each of the parsley, chives and onion mixed with 175 g (6 oz) butter, 225 g (8 oz) of cream cheese, 1 teaspoon of French mustard, a pinch of caraway, 2 tablespoons of paprika and the 2 chopped anchovies all mixed with 2 tablespoons of beer. In Budapest it is often made with a soft sheeps' milk curd cheese.

Jambon Persille de Bourgogne

This is a regional speciality seen in the *charcuteries* in

Burgundy. The ham, which is simmered with parsley in local white wine—perhaps Aligote or an inexpensive Chablis—looks like a pink and green brawn. It is a 'must' in Dijon for lunch on Easter Sunday.

Soak a 0.9-1.2 kg (2-2½ lb) piece of ham in cold water for 2 or 3 hours to remove some of the salt. Meanwhile put a shin bone, 2 calves' feet, 2 bay leaves, 1 onion, 6 peppercorns, some fresh thyme, and plenty of tarragon and parsley in a large pan, and add a bottle of dry white wine and a little water so everything is well covered. Bring it to the boil, then reduce the heat and let it simmer for 3 hours with the lid on. Add the piece of ham and let it simmer till tender in the stock.

Chop the ham in chunks, meat and fat together, and press it gently into a glass bowl. Strain the stock through a fine sieve. When it is cold lift all the fat from the surface, wasting a little of the jellied stock if necessary to be sure all the fat has been taken off it. Then clear the stock with 1 beaten egg white and 1 crushed egg shell and pour it through a filter to give a good clear jellying stock (see page 98). Pour a little of the stock over the ham just to moisten it, and chill the rest in the refrigerator. When it is just setting, stir in 1 tablespoon of tarragon-flavoured white wine vinegar and 150 ml (¼ pint) dry white wine, as well as a good quantity of finely chopped fresh parsley. Pour all this over the ham and let it set in a cool place.

Three pigs' feet might be used if the calves' feet are unobtainable.

Lincolnshire stuffed chine, sometimes called the sheep-shearing chine, is still seen in East Anglian butchers' shops, and is popular for country suppers. Like the *jambon persille de bourgogne* it is a delicate pink and green dish. The chine (Fr. *échine*) is a special country cut from the back of the pig, not found readily in other parts of the country. The pork, which is salted, is stuffed with chopped herbs—parsley , marjoram, leek—which are pressed into slits in the chine. It is tied in a cloth and boiled, then eaten cold with mustard.

Lancashire Brawn*

Lancashire farmhouse brawn is made with half a pig's head, which is usually a bargain even today and is often included with a side of pork which has been bought for freezing. It will make several large pudding basins of brawn; the whole secret is in long slow simmering.

Get the butcher to prepare and chop the half head in chunks which will fit in a saucepan. Put it in a pan with water to cover. If the pig's head has been salted bring it to the boil, then throw away the water and put in fresh water to cover. Add a good pinch of nutmeg and 2 bay leaves, 6 cloves, a strip of lemon rind and 12 peppercorns. Bring it to the boil and let it simmer, gently bubbling, with a lid on for about 4 hours until the meat can be slipped easily off the bone.

In Lancashire the pig's tongue and heart are often put with the other meat, chopped and included in the brawn. When the meat is cooked it is removed with a spoon. Chop some of it in chunks, throwing away any off-beat or gristly bits. Mince the rest of the meat, then put it back in the strained stock with 150 ml (¼ pint) of wine vinegar. Boil it up and pour it into basins. When cold it sets in a jelly. It can be set in little earthenware crocks or in one large dish, then turned out on to cracked ice to make a glossy centrepiece for the cold table. It used to be the mainstay of Edwardian country-house breakfasts along with game pie and devilled partridge.

Fromage de Tête en Salade

Something very similar to our traditional farmhouse brawn is sold by most French *charcutiers* in slices marinated in oil and vinegar with coarsely chopped parsley and onion. It makes an excellent *hors d'oeuvre*. The vinaigrette sauce to go on it is made by chopping a small onion finely, and adding ½ teaspoon of French mustard with oil and wine vinegar in the proportions of 5 parts oil to one of vinegar. Cover the thin slices of brawn with this and before serving sprinkle them with plenty of chopped parsley.

Museau de Boeuf en Salade*

A popular dish in French *charcuteries* is simply an ox cheek cooked slowly till tender, sliced when cold and mixed with

111

chopped parsley and an oil and vinegar dressing. It is also a good way of reviving rather dull cold meat.

Lapin en Gelée au Vin Blanc et au Serpolet

Bone a small wild rabbit, one which will yield about 450 g (1 lb) of meat. Put the pieces in a deep dish with 300 ml (½ pint) of dry white wine. Add 1 tablespoon of finely chopped onion, 1 tablespoon chopped parsley, 1 teaspoon of chopped tarragon, 2 sprigs of wild thyme and 1 tablespoon of chopped lemon balm (*melissa*) if available. Marinate it overnight. Cook the rabbit bones in a pressure cooker for about 30 minutes with salt, pepper, soup vegetables, herbs and enough water to make 600 ml (1 pint) of stock. Strain, and stir in the contents of a 15 g (½ oz) packet of gelatine. Add the strained marinade. Put the rabbit pieces in a glass pudding basin or terrine, pour the stock over, and stand the basin in a water bath. Cook it in a slow oven, 150°C (300°F)/Gas 2 for 2 hours. Chill. Serve it straight from the pudding basin or terrine.

Dry cider can be used instead of dry white wine but then the flavour and also the name of the dish is slightly different.

Grav-Mackerel*

Gravlax is a great Scandinavian delicacy, a famous way of pickling fresh salmon. However, as the chairman of the prestigious House of Sandeman, Timothy Sandeman, explained to me recently this delicious technique can also be used for pickled mackerel. Here is his recipe for grav-mackerel.

'You need a large mackerel which ideally you get your fishmonger to fillet for you. You then rub approximately 1 teaspoonful of salt into each fillet, the same quantity of sugar and grind a good deal of black pepper over the fillets. You then take dry dill, or in the unlikely event that you have it a good bunch of fresh dill—you want a fairly liberal sprinkling of the dry dill. Ideally, but not completely

112

necessary, sprinkle a little dry sherry on the two fillets, or, alternatively, a small drop of brandy. Put the fillets together and leave them for about 6 hours one way up and 6 hours the other way up, obviously in a cool place. Then slice thinly and eat as smoked salmon.'

Timothy Sandeman himself only leaves the fillets for a mere 2 hours on each side but says this could be too raw for most people.

Faggots*

Faggots (and haslets or 'savoury ducks') are well liked by country people all over Britain and according to some scholars are of Roman origin, though the use of caul fat or 'veiling' suggests an even earlier date. Some are made with pig's liver, others with pig's fry with added pig's liver. The *crépinettes* or *gayettes* sold by French pork butchers are very similar to faggots.

Pig's fry is now almost a regional delicacy. It is very popular in East Anglia and some parts of Yorkshire but almost unknown elsewhere and is often difficult to buy. It consists in pig's kidney, liver, heart, pork belly and melt all cut up small. These are often rolled in flour, seasoned, then cooked with chopped onion, pork dripping and a little water in the oven. Pig's liver will have to be used if the fry is unobtainable.

Caul fat is the lacy fat from near the kidneys sometimes called flead, or fleed fat, or leaf, or veiling, or 'kell' fat in different parts of the country. It is a familiar sight in French and Belgian *charcuteries* and is often used in making pâté.

To make faggots cut up 450 g (1 lb) of proper pig's fry in smallish pieces together with a little extra pig's liver, and put it in a pan with 100 g (4 oz) peeled chopped onion. Cover it with cold water, and bring almost to the boil very slowly and gently. Simmer until the meat is partly cooked, then take the pan off the heat and let it cool. Now mince the meat and onions, saving the liquid in the pan for the gravy. Add salt, pepper and chopped sage leaves to the mince and enough soft white breadcrumbs to make a nice, not too wet, mixture. Mix it well. Put some caul fat or veiling in a basin in warm water for a few minutes, then pull out pieces to wrap each

113

faggot in. With floured hands, form the mixture into small neat balls or cakes. Cover each with a piece of caul fat. It is this that makes all the difference to the flavour.

Put the faggots in greased fireproof dishes or baking tins closely packed and bake them in a moderate oven, 180°C (350°F)/Gas 4, for about 45 minutes. They are often served hot with mashed potatoes and gravy but are very good cold.

The gravy is made by melting a tablespoon of dripping and adding a dessertspoon of flour. Fry till brown. Stir this into the reserved liquid in the pan and heat, stirring, until it thickens. Some cooks add a little cold tea to improve the colour.

Haslet is similar but is made in one piece, rather like a terrine.

Gayettes (French Faggots)*

From Montignac in the Dordogne, these are eaten cold in France, though they are also excellent hot. They smell delicious and are often baked in a huge flat roasting tin.

Dice 450 g (1 lb) pig's liver and 350 g (12 oz) of pickled pork belly (from the butcher) without the skin. Crush and pound 1 garlic clove with 1 teaspoon salt, 1 teaspoon black pepper, and 1 pinch of allspice (*les 4 épices*). Mix this with the meats and put them through the mincer. Form the mixture into neat balls or cakes with floured hands, and wrap each in a piece of caul fat. Pack them side by side in a baking tin. Bake in a moderate oven, 180°C (350°F)/Gas 4, for about 30 minutes until the tops are brown.

TRACKLEMENTS

A WELL-MADE PÂTÉ or terrine can make a perfect meal just with a bottle of wine and some freshly baked bread. Or perhaps with a bowl of hot jacket potatoes and a piece of butter . . . or pickled gherkins . . . or a simple salad.

I have used the old English word *tracklements*, for want of another, to describe some of the things that go with pâtés and terrines, galantines and mousses, and that are pleasant to eat with them, or pretty to serve around them, or both. Though almost vanished from everyday English speech the word is still used fairly commonly in Staffordshire, Shropshire and the Welsh border counties.

Fresh Brown Soda Bread

Old-fashioned soda bread has a robust country taste which goes well with farmhouse pâté.

Mix 450 g (1 lb) of coarse ground wheat flour (such as Allinson's) with 450 g (1 lb) of plain strong flour. Add 2 teaspoons of bread soda (bicarbonate of soda) and 1 teaspoon of salt. Then rub in 100 g (4 oz) of butter.

Make a well in the middle of the now crumbly mixture and gradually add something over 450 ml (¾ pint) of thick sour milk—or of the buttermilk sold nowadays by most milkmen. Mix it to make a soft but not runny dough. Knead it into a ball as lightly as possible with floured hands—it is best done quickly and gently. Put the dough on a floured baking sheet. Flatten it out in a circle 2 cm (1½ in) thick and make a cross through the middle so as to let the Devil out and also to divide it into four. Put it in the oven without delay. Bake it in a really hot oven, 220°C (450°F)/Gas 7, and reduce the heat after about 25 minutes to 180°C (350°F)/Gas 4 for a further 15 minutes or so to finish cooking it. Knock on the back of the loaf with your knuckles. If it gives a hollow sound it is done.

Bread, Oil and Garlic

A long crisp loaf, some cloves of raw garlic and ripe green olive oil with a fruity flavour—preferably from Tuscany—go perfectly with red wine and chicken liver pâté. Peel the garlic, rub it on the bread, dip this in the olive oil, and savour it slowly. Some Italians eat this with their eyes shut, the better to appreciate an olive oil of good vintage in its full subtlety.

Hot Garlic Bread

Take long French loaves and make slanting cuts in them about 2 cm (1½ in) apart. Don't cut through to the bottom; the loaves must stay in one piece. For each loaf, finely chop two garlic cloves and mix with 75 g (3 oz) of butter. Put a lump of this in each cut. Wrap the loaves in foil like a parcel, then polythene bags, seal and store in the freezer. Before serving take off the polythene bags and put the frozen foil-wrapped loaves for 15 minutes in a moderate oven, 180°C (350°F)/Gas 4. Turn back the foil, and turn up the oven to very hot, 230°C (450°F)/Gas 8. Leave the loaves in until they are crusty—about 10 minutes. Serve them hot from the oven in their wrappings.

Garlic Toast

A speciality of the Carlton Hotel, Johannesburg, this is superb with all kinds of pâtés and cold meats. I have never seen it elsewhere. You need some good rye bread cut in very thin slices and covered sparingly with garlic butter (see above). Put the slices in a very hot oven, 230°C (450°F)/Gas 8, for a few minutes just before serving.

118

Devilled Biscuits

Devilled biscuits were a great Victorian tavern delicacy. Delicious with kipper pâté, they used to be served hot in a folded napkin between courses at dinner, perhaps to make one thirsty and encourage drinking. It is best to use thin wine or water biscuits.

Make some Devil butter by mixing together 40 g (1½ oz) butter, a saltspoon of Cayenne pepper, and a saltspoon of dry mustard powder. Dip each biscuit twice in hot beer, then spread them with Devil butter. Place on a hot baking sheet in a slow oven, 150°C (300°F)/Gas 2, bake until crisp again, and serve piping hot.

Dorset Knobs and Suffolk Rusks

Dorset knobs and Suffolk rusks are both crisp, dry and crunchy, excellent to eat with pâtés and terrines, very popular in the two districts where they are made but virtually unknown elsewhere.

A Dorset knob is a sort of rusk which is made by hand at Morecombelake, a small village 4 miles outside Bridport. Mr Keith Moores and his cousin Ivor are the only people producing them now and they use the same recipe as their grandfather, Saw, who used to make them on a farm outside Stoke Mills about a hundred years ago. They think their recipe may be the old one which was fashionable in nearby Weymouth when George III came there for the bathing in 1789, dipping his royal person into the briny to the strains of the National Anthem, and later, we believe, to 'Rule Britannia'. 'They used to be made in the old faggot oven,' says Mr Keith Moores in his soft Dorset voice, 'using the receding heat to dry them out and make rusks, didn't they cousin? We make them by hand and cannot do enough. It is difficult to get a machine that will do it without changing the recipe.' His cousin Ivor agrees with him. Farm workers round Morecombelake have always eaten Dorset knobs for breakfast before milking, and the old Dorset people still dip them in their tea. They may be had by post from the West End Dairy, 35 West Bridport Street, Bridport, Dorset, from

Messrs Fortnum and Mason, Piccadilly, London W1, or Messrs Harrods, Knightsbridge, London SW1.

Suffolk rusks are not dissimilar. People eat them buttered for breakfast and the drier they are the better they like them. The rusks used to be made in the old Suffolk brick ovens which were something like large boxes heated by burning faggots or dry gorse inside them. The door was the only outlet, and when the oven was hot enough, the fire was scraped out and the bread set in. The weekly joint was often baked in the back of the oven behind the bread, and the Suffolk rusks, which only took about ten minutes, were baked in front. Bits of charcoal and embers from the fire sometimes stuck to them, giving extra flavour.

John Tester and Jonathan Wright, the Woodbridge bakers, are famous for their hand-made bread and Suffolk rusks and this is their recipe:

Mix 40 g (1½ oz) plain flour with 20 g (¾ oz) of baking powder. Then rub in 100 g (4 oz) of butter and 100 g (4 oz) of lard. Stir in 150 ml (just over ¼ pint) of milk, a beaten egg, 7 g (¼ oz) of salt and 15 g (½ oz) of sugar. Mix to bind. Roll the dough out to a thickness of 1 cm (½ in), and then cut it in rounds with 5 cm (2 in) cutter. Leave the rusks for about 30 minutes in the warm bakery or kitchen, then bake them in a pre-heated hot oven, 200°C (400°F)/Gas 6, for 20 minutes.

When the rusks are cool enough to handle, split them in two and bake them again for about 10 minutes in the hot oven until golden brown.

Cornichons

These are pickled gherkins, or ridge cucumbers soured by lactic fermentation as is sauerkraut. They have dill leaves added and are called dill pickles in the U.S. and *salzgurken* in Germany. They appear in France in bourgeois restaurants, usually in a stoneware jar steeped in their own pickle, and are lifted out with a large pair of wooden tongs. They are eaten with pâté.

Wash 10 small fat ridge cucumbers and pack them into a large glass jar—about a 4 litre (1 gallon) capacity. They should be put in the jar in layers with fresh vine leaves or morello cherry leaves and some pieces of dill. Sprinkle them

120

with salt and black peppercorns (about 7 g (¼ oz) of these per large jar), continuing till the jar is full, and also about 25 g (1 oz) of dark rye bread broken in little pieces. This is for the fermentation. Pour in cold water to cover. Put a piece of greaseproof paper lightly on top of the jar and keep it for 8-10 days in a warm spot, for instance on a sunny windowsill. Then tie down the jar and store it in a cool place. The cornichons are ready for use.

Stuffed Eggs

Hard boil 6 eggs, plunge them into cold water, shell them when cold. Halve them sideways with a serrated knife, remove the yolks, and if necessary cut a small piece off the end of the empty egg whites so they will stand upright. Mash the egg yolks with a little French mustard, oil, pepper, salt and lemon juice to make a smooth paste. Add about 1 teaspoon of curry powder, 1 tablespoon of grated cheese and, if liked, 1 good teaspoon of anchovy paste. Pile the mixture back in the egg whites. Garnish each with a stoned black olive.

Blue Cucumber

Cut both ends off a fairly small cucumber. Core it with an apple corer from either end, removing the seeds and middle. Use a small knife too if necessary but be careful not to break the shell. Stuff it with a cheese mixture, half cream cheese and half mashed blue cheese well mixed. Chill it, then cut the cucumber in thin slices.

Stuffed Tomatoes

Tomatoes are very good stuffed with shredded celeriac in mayonnaise. Celeriac, or turnip-rooted celery, is primarily a winter vegetable which will keep for a long time in the kitchen cupboard. It may weigh up to almost 2 kg (4 lb). Cut the tops off some tomatoes to make a 'lid', and scoop out the centres. Peel off a section of the brown fibrous skin of the celeriac, then shred some of the cut surface, either with an ordinary kitchen grater or, better still, with a mandoline. Toss the shredded celeriac in a mild lemon mayonnaise and use it to stuff the tomatoes.

Other Garnishes

Seedless green grapes, usually from Cyprus, are available in July and August, and they can be frozen. They look well on a dish garnished with aspic. Mushrooms—rinsed, patted dry in a cloth, and then sliced right across in thin pieces so they look like the silhouette of a mushroom—make another pretty garnish when arranged in heaps on the cold dish. Crisply fried thin rashers of bacon, served cold, make a good garnish for some dishes, alternated perhaps with green grapes. Both black and green olives are useful too.

Potato Salad

This is delicious with galantines and pâtés, and excellent with the Hungarian spiced hare (page 63). It must be mixed hot.

I) The firm waxy texture of new potatoes is most appropriate for salads. Boil them, and as soon as they are cool enough to handle slice them and dress them *while still warm* with a classic oil and vinegar dressing—4 tablespoons of olive oil to 1 of wine vinegar. Add chopped chives or spring onion tops, and slices of salami and black olives if you like.

II) Plain boiled cold potatoes cut in chunks are delicious, too, when rolled in aioli, or garlic mayonnaise (page 123). This can be very good with *pâté en croûte,* meat pies, brawn, the cold turkey with two pâtes (page 82) and of course with the boar's head (page 80).

Salade de Pissenlits au Lard

A spring salad made from young dandelion shoots which are blanched under stones or flowerpots. Very popular in northeast France, and delicious with a coarse-cut country pâté. Chicory may be used instead. The salad is mixed at table with crisp snips of hot bacon.

Wash 450 g (1 lb) of young blanched dandelion leaves (or two heads of chicory) in plenty of water to remove any grit. Cut off the bottom; just keep the pale leaves. Rub the salad bowl with a piece of cut garlic, add the salad greens and sprinkle with 2 dashes of wine vinegar.

Dice 225 g (8 oz) of 'green' streaky bacon and soften it in a small greased pan for about 10 minutes. Pour it all, bacon and bacon fat, over the salad. Garnish with a chopped hard-boiled egg.

Salade de Champignons

Wash 225 g (8 oz) mushrooms and cut off the sandy ends of the stalks. Slice the mushrooms thinly to look like the silhouette of a mushroom. Pat them dry in a tea towel. Mix them with a dressing of 2 tablespoons of olive oil to 1 dessertspoon lemon juice, salt and pepper, and plenty of chopped parsley.

Salade Rouge

Sliced red paprika peppers, without the seeds, and cut in thin shreds, are laid on sliced tomatoes on a shallow dish with oil, vinegar, salt and pepper, a little chopped chives or garlic and some sweet basil.

Aioli

Aioli, or *skordalia* as the Greeks call it, is that lovely garlic mayonnaise so popular round the Mediterranean with cold meats, hard-boiled eggs, etc. It is delicious on potato salad and easier to make than ordinary mayonnaise. Mash a table-spoonful of soft white breadcrumbs with 3 peeled chopped garlic cloves and a little oil to make it into a paste. Then add an egg yolk and a little salt and pepper. Pour 450 ml (¾ pint) of olive oil into a small jug. Gradually trickle the oil into the mixture, drop by drop at first, beating it with a wooden spoon. As the mixture thickens into a mayonnaise the oil may be added more quickly, but do not go too fast as it might curdle. If it does, break an egg yolk into another basin and gradually beat in the curdled aioli. Add the juice of 1 lemon and it is done.

Cumberland Sauce

Delicious with pâté, cold venison, ham or brawn.

Simmer the shredded peel of 2 lemons and 4 oranges in water for about 5 minutes. Drain. Put the peel in a pan with 150 ml (¼ pint) of red wine, 1 dessertspoon French mustard, 450 g (1 lb) redcurrant jelly, 2 tablespoons wine vinegar, 2 tablespoons sugar, and salt and pepper. Simmer for 30 minutes, then bottle and seal. It keeps for months.

Cold Mustard Sauce

This was served with brawn in Elizabethan England. It is simply mustard powder moistened with thick cream, and then with much more thick cream added, quantities to your liking.

Mayonnaise

When egg whites have been used to clarify stock and make it into aspic, the yolks left over may well be used to make mayonnaise. Serve this with, for instance, the terrine of fresh salmon (page 54), a boar's head (page 80), or cold turkey with two pâtés (page 82).

It is not difficult to make real mayonnaise at home which is mild and creamy in flavour. Beat up 2 egg yolks, the juice of 1 lemon, and a pinch each of salt and pepper in a small basin with a wooden spoon. Pour 450 ml (¾ pint) of olive oil into a small jug, and add this drop by drop, at first beating it as you go. As the egg thickens and becomes pale and creamy the oil can be added more quickly and trickled into the mixture towards the end, but if the oil is added too fast it will curdle. If it does curdle simply beat up another egg yolk in another basin and then little by little stir in your curdled mayonnaise just as you stir in the oil.

Do not put home-made mayonnaise in the refrigerator or the freezer as the change in temperature sometimes makes it curdle. It is better to cover it with a plate or basin and leave it somewhere cool away from draughts.

HERBS AND SPICES

A FEW FLAVOURED HERBS are absolutely essential to good cooking, and make all the difference to a plain dish. Most people have now realized, however, that the little cardboard drums and small glass bottles of dried herbs, though sold everywhere, are often stale and that the expensive contents taste and smell of very little.

Ideally one should grow one's own herbs in the garden or on the kitchen windowsill, drying them in summer for later use, but this is not always possible. Most fresh herbs freeze very well however, keeping their green colour and much more aroma and flavour than those that have been dried. Even a very small bunch of fresh herbs from a shop can be screwed up in kitchen foil, labelled, and stored in the freezer for instant use. Frozen parsley does not need to be chopped; it can be scrunched up in the fingers while still frozen and used at once as a garnish.

Spices should be bought in small quantities for they do not retain their flavour, even when well cooked. Just as black pepper has a more subtle flavour when freshly ground, so most other spices not only taste stronger but very different when freshly ground or grated. A kitchen grater, a coffee grinder, a spare wooden pepper mill or an electric mixer can be helpful.

Allspice (and Les 4 Épices)

This used to be called Jamaica pepper as it comes from a West Indian tree, but it is now grown in other tropical countries as well as Jamaica. It has purple berries which when dried look like large peppercorns. They are used whole to flavour stock—about 6 may be added to a piece of salt brisket or a 1.35 kg (3 lb) piece of gammon when boiling.

Whole allspice berries are also put in the brine for pickled herrings.

Allspice was so called because the ground berries were once thought to taste like cinnamon, cloves and nutmeg mixed. This is similar to the classic *les 4 èspices*—a mixture used in France almost as widely as the *bouquet garni*. French cooks mix their own, though in Paris it can be bought ready-made in jars. The proportions vary but are often 7 parts pepper to 1 part each of nutmeg, ground cloves and ground cinnamon. Sometimes ginger is substituted for the cinnamon. It is much used in game pâtés and casseroles. Allspice may be substituted, but then white pepper should be added too.

Unfortunately *les 4 épices* is often confused with the mixed spices sold in cartons which, though very good, are totally different and intended for fruit cakes and boiled puddings.

Anchovy

This of course is the small fish of the herring family which is fished with lamps in the Mediterranean and the south European Atlantic. Anchovies are used either pickled in salt or preserved in oil. Those in tins are usually filleted. They are used in a Melton Mowbray pork pie.

Bay Leaves (Lauris nobilis)

The leaves are laid on top of some pâtés, terrines and mousses as a garnish and for flavour. Bay leaves are one of the herbs of a *bouquet garni* and are much used in cooking. They were used to make the classic hero's crown in ancient times, and look very pretty whether round the head of Caesar, or the Emperor Napoleon, or laid on top of a chicken mousse. The Greeks call the plant Daphne after the nymph who was changed into a small bay tree when she was in imminent danger of rape. The leaves are much used in Greece for putting in the clean laundry, and laid in the linen cupboard. They give a sweet scent to clean sheets.

Capers

These are used as a garnish with bay leaves on top of pâtés, with or without aspic, and are stirred into some chicken liver pâtés, for sharpness, as a contrast in flavours. They are really the flower buds of the caper plant and are used when pickled in vinegar. They grow wild in Cyprus. Some people pickle small nasturtium seeds in the same way as a substitute.

Chives

One of the classic *fines herbes*, and pleasant, too, in salad. They look like dolls' house onions, and are an easily grown perennial from which one snips the green tops, with scissors, as required. They cannot be dried but they do freeze well for winter when the tops have died down.

Clarified Butter

Clarified butter is used to seal the top of jars of English potted meats and fish, thus excluding the contents from contact with the air, in the same way as lard is used on French pâtés. Butter, which contains milk solids, is clarified to get rid of them.

Put the butter in a saucepan on a low heat. Skim the foam off the surface, gently, as it rises. When the butter becomes very clear and particles of sediment sink to the bottom of the pan, and the foam stops rising, take if off the heat. Strain it through a fine sieve, gently, so as not to disturb the sediment in the bottom of the pan. Let it cool and set before using it. 225 g (8 oz) of butter takes 15-20 minutes to clarify, but a large quantity can take about an hour. It must never be heated enough to make it darken in colour.

Coriander Seeds

They have a fresh smell like sandalwood and a taste of burnt orange peel, good with roast lamb and pork. Crushed coriander seeds are sometimes laid on a duck pâté with a bay leaf, pieces of orange or of orange peel, usually with aspic. The seeds are also used in the marinade for potted venison.

Dripping

Duck or goose dripping is delicious to spread on brown bread but is usually too liquid even when chilled. It is best to mix a little melted lard with it, just enough to make it spreadable, then chill it. Add salt if liked. In peasant homes in the Dordogne the goose dripping is spread on thick slices of country bread and eaten with a bit of cold meat. It is also used a great deal in Southern France and central Europe for cooking. Indeed the cooking of the Perigord district in particular is done virtually entirely in goose fat, duck fat or walnut oil. It is, as someone said, *'sans beurre et sans re-prôches'*.

Spiced lard is a Danish speciality and is delicious on *smørrebrød* which will be topped with liver pâté. Melt the lard or pork dripping. Fry a little minced onion and a little crushed sage, or a very small amount of crushed bay leaf, in the hot fat very gently without browning the onion. Then strain and chill it before using. Spread dark bread with the spiced pork fat, top it with liver pâté, and garnish with chopped aspic or a slice of gherkin.

Garlic

'Very few people are indifferent to either the aroma or flavour of garlic,' as Alice B. Toklas wrote in *Aromas and Flavours of Past and Present*. 'One is affected favourably or unfavourably. It may have been the odour of garlic with which Henry James was greeted when he went to call upon George Eliot for the first time and which he later described as the right odour in the wrong place. Though I had not tasted garlic as a young girl when I read this, it had the alluring mysterious quality of the unknown for some years after. Then I was asked to a lunch party at a schoolmate's. Upon my return my mother asked me if I had enjoyed myself.

Inexpressibly, I breathed. For lunch there was steak smothered in garlic. It was to be a long time before I was to know such rapture and surprise again. For garlic was not admitted in my mother's kitchen, nor did she consider my enjoyment of the strong flavour of salmon, sweetbreads, brussels sprouts, all cheeses, caviar, the onion family including garlic, and wine, natural or commendable in her young daughter. But these are all as enjoyable to me today as they were then . . .'

Juniper Berries

These are of course one of the ingredients used to flavour gin, but they are also very popular abroad in game stuffings, for marinades, and in pâtés and terrines. They are often used with wild boar, pork or venison and in Switzerland are added to a *choucroûte garnie*. In Belgium larks, thrushes, and sometimes quails are preserved whole in little potting pots and flavoured with juniper berries. They are also an indispensable ingredient of the famous *rognons sautées Liegeoises*. In Britain they were once used in beef stews.

Squash or crush them before use. Gin can often be added to increase the taste. They are the berries, blue when ripe, of a prickly bush, *juniperis communis*. Those bought here, dried, from herbalists and grocers usually have much less flavour than the ones gathered in late summer on the hills in Greece and Provence. The berries take three years to ripen and one finds ripe and unripe berries on the same female bush.

Mace and Nutmeg

Mace is the membrane surrounding the shell of the nutmeg and has much the same taste but is more 'refined'. It is more expensive. It comes in little orange lacy flakes or 'blades', useful in pale or clear dishes as it can be removed before serving whereas a nutmeg powder could not.

Nutmeg is much used in English potted meats and in Italian cooking. It tastes much better when bought whole and ground freshly before using. The little boxes of nutmeg powder are pale shadows of the real thing.

According to Mrs Beeton in the original 1861 edition of her *Book of Household Management* it 'is a native of the Moluccas and was long kept from being spread in other places by the monopolizing spirit of the Dutch, who endeavoured to keep it wholly to themselves by eradicating it from every other island . . . The plant, through the enterprise of the British, has now found its way into Penang and Bencoolen where it flourishes and produces well. It has also been tried to be naturalized in the West Indies, and it bears fruit all the year round.'

Pepper

Black pepper is made by picking the berries of the pepper vine when they are green and drying them in the sun. It is best bought as peppercorns and ground as required. The ready powdered kind is often mixed with something else and has—perceptibly—lost its special aroma. The pepper vine grows in tropical countries such as Sri-Lanka, Madagascar and Brazil, places with a warm wet climate.

Some pâtés, *pâtés de foies de volaille en gelée* for instance, have whole black peppercorns, lightly crushed but entire, laid thickly across the top. The peppercorns are crushed roughly with a rolling pin or kitchen weight, but not ground, and then spread over the top. The pâté is covered with foil and left 2-3 hours before cooking. The aroma and flavour of the peppercorns will penetrate the pâté, and being so dark they contrast appetizingly with the very pale chicken livers. Most people don't eat them. A little aspic is usually run over the top of the cold pâté to give a shiny finish.

Green pepper—*Poivre vert*—also comes from the pepper vine. The berries are picked when green and soft and unripe as before, but are then packed in tins. These fresh or green peppercorns, soft and subtle, are now freely available here in tins, and can also be had freeze-dried, when they can be used as a spice. Even the liquid in which the tinned green peppercorns are packed can be used with care as a flavouring. They are now very fashionable not only on grilled steaks, but in pâtés, terrines and so on and in the *farce* for galantines.

White pepper is said to have a different flavour from black, hotter but less aromatic. It is used in dishes which would be discoloured by the black pepper. Like black pepper and green pepper it is made from the berries of the pepper vine but they are left on the plant until they are ripe. They then turn a bright orange red and are specially prepared, the outside red husks being rubbed off.

Red pepper, Cayenne pepper, chilli pepper, paprika pepper and the small pointed **pickling peppers** all come from a totally different plant, the *capsicum*. It is of a completely different genus and grows under totally different conditions from the pepper vine. The name is confusing.

Small fresh green chilli 'peppers', which can be very pungent or very mild, are often used nowadays as a garnish on commerically made pâtés. They look attractive set in aspic on top of it but are not meant to be eaten. Fresh scarlet chillies, mostly chokingly hot, very pungent indeed, and inedible, are sometimes used too.

The tinned **Spanish pimentos,** brilliant scarlet, mild and delicate in flavour, are also red 'peppers' but make a delicious and very edible garnish.

Pistachio

The pale green kernel of a nut which grows in clusters on small trees among the almonds and olives around the Mediterranean. They are, or were, popular in galantines, sausages, and *pâtés en croûte,* for their delicate taste and pretty colouring but are evidently less used now than they were in the last century. They are the green nuts found in good nougat, and are used to make pistachio ice cream. They keep will but are rather expensive.

Salt

There has been a kind of snobbery for some years among the fancier domestic cooks about the necessity of having grey French sea salt, *le gros sel,* rather than our own coarse salt in crystals from Northwich, or sea salt from Maldon, which is better, prettier and has more flavour.

Saltpetre, or potassium nitrate, can be bought from a pharmacy. This is what gives that attractive pink colour to boiled ham, or tongues and salt beef—without it they would be grey. It absorbs moisture and so stops the pickle from becoming wet—too much hardens the meat, too little and it becomes slimy. Country people used it in my childhood for curing rabbit skins—which were nailed out on a board, fur inwards, and rubbed with saltpetre till dry and hard.

Smoked salt is primarily an American condiment. The salt is usually blue-grey and flavoured with hickory smoke. It is used with grills to heighten the smokey taste of some meat and fish dishes. It is sold in small jars.

Truffles

The black French truffle from the Perigord is much used in fashionable French pâtés for flavour and as an elegant black garnish. Unless very fresh the truffle is probably not worth the money. Those in tins have little flavour. Some chefs use a 'truffle substitute'—rumoured to be of black plastic—for the elaborate garnishes and decorations sometimes applied to hams, turkeys and joints of beef. A fresh black truffle, should you be fortunate enough to have one, will keep for months if put in a jar with a little brandy. At the Mirabelle restaurant in London M. Jean Drees, the chef, keeps his truffles in a locked cabinet and carries the keys on his person.

According to Brillat-Savarin, in *La Physiologie du Gout*, 'Whoever says "truffles" utters a great word which arouses erotic and gastronomic memories among the skirted sex, and memories gastronomic and erotic among the bearded sex. This dual distinction is due to the fact that the noble tuber is not only considered delicious to the taste, but is also believed to foster powers the exercise of which is extremely pleasurable.

'The origin of the truffle is unknown; it is found, but nobody knows of its birth or growth. The greatest minds have pondered over it; at one time it was thought that its seed had been discovered, and it was declared that truffles might be sown at will. Vain efforts and illusory promises! No

136

harvest was ever reaped from that sowing; and perhaps that is no great misfortune; for since the price of truffles is partly a matter of caprice, they might well be held in less esteem if they were available in quantity and cheap.

'"Rejoice, my dear," I said one day to Madame de V——; "a loom has just been shown to the Society for Encouragement on which it will be possible to manufacture superb lace for practically nothing.'

'"Why," the lady replied, with an air of supreme indifference, "if lace were cheap, do you think anybody would want to wear such rubbish?"'

Index